The Amazing Life of

Jesus Christ

Part One

BIG
DREAM
MINISTRIES

His Preexistence,
Birth, and Early Ministry

© 2017 by Big Dream Ministries

No part of *The Amazing Life of Jesus Christ*, whether audio, video, or print, may be reproduced in any form without written permission from Big Dream Ministries, Inc. P.O. Box 324, 12460 Crabapple Road, Suite 202, Alpharetta, Georgia, 30004.

ISBN 10: 1-932199-52-7
ISBN 13: 978-1-932199-52-9

Cover design by Melissa Swanson
Cover photo from iStock Photos
Creative Team: Terry Behimer, Pat Reinheimer, and Leslie Strader

Scripture structure and organization taken from *One Perfect Life: The Complete Story of the Lord Jesus* by John MacArthur. Copyright © 2012 by John MacArthur. Used by permission of Thomas Nelson. www.thomasnelson.com.

Unless otherwise identified, all Scripture quotations in this publication are taken from the New American Standard Bible (NASB). © The Lockman Foundation 1960, 1962, 1963, 1968, 1971, 1972, 1973, 1975, 1977, 1995.

Printed in the United States

2 3 4 5 6 7 8 9 10 / 23 22 21 20 19 18

TABLE OF CONTENTS

JESUS IS AMAZING

In history and religion, there is no more controversial or captivating figure, no one who has made a greater impact on individuals or institutions, than Jesus of Nazareth. Jesus is amazing! Every word on every page of Scripture proclaims this truth. The Gospel writers were given the inspired privilege of breathing literary life into the Word made flesh. And we get to bask in the glory.

So much of the life of Jesus is familiar, whether you grew up in church or not. Who hasn't heard of the One who turned water into wine, walked on top of the waves, and fed thousands with a few fish and bits of bread? Or how He cast out demons and healed the incurable diseases of the day—even the incurable conditions of *our* day? Blindness, paralysis, and leprosy didn't stand a chance at the hand of the Great Physician. He cured with compassion. He restored life and hope.

And when He taught, Jesus' words were more than moving, beyond simply radical thinking. Every time He opened His mouth, Jesus spoke life-changing truth, and it fell on ears and hearts like rain on parched land. Stray sheep heard the voice of the Good Shepherd at last. Following Him, however, was another story.

It is all of these things and more that we will examine together in *The Amazing Life of Jesus Christ*. Rather than rushing through the "Sunday school stories" some know by heart, we will slow our pace. These words are treasures and so we will hold them tightly, turn them over in our hands, and watch them sparkle in the light.

The permanence of Scripture offers us an extraordinary opportunity: we can carefully (and joyfully!) explore the life of the One who left the beauty, perfection, and glory of heaven to *"be made like his brethren in all things, so that he might become a merciful and faithful high priest in things pertaining to God, to make propitiation for the sins of the people."* (Hebrews 2:17)

Pray for eyes to see Him as He was on earth—a Man fully human and perfectly divine, and as He is today—seated at His Father's right hand, His work completed, waiting to return.

Thanks be to God for His indescribable gift! (2 Corinthians 9:15)

With joy,

Leslie Strader

ABOUT THIS STUDY

Theme:
Instead of focusing on one book in the Gospels, *The Amazing Life of Jesus Christ* weaves together Scripture primarily from Matthew, Mark, Luke, and John in chronological order, journeying from the preexistence of Jesus to His future return. At the same time, this study will focus on a particular aspect of Jesus' character each week. From Son of Man to King of Kings, we will slow down the Gospel story and examine the teaching, miracles, words, and heart of the One who came to save.

Teaching:
The weekly teacher presentations will offer additional information that will enhance the understanding of Christ's life on earth. Each section of Scripture is unfolded in a way that will draw your heart into the story and encourage you to sense the great impact Jesus had on those around Him and the power of the battle that began even as He was an infant.

Introduction:
To help calibrate the timeline and set your mind, take time to read through the introduction at the beginning of each week. This will give you an overview of what you will be studying and orient you to where we are in the life of Christ.

Maps:
Where relevant to the content of the passage, maps are included to give an additional visual connection to where Jesus is, how far He might have traveled, and where He's going.

Memory Verses:
Each week begins with a verse from the passage of Scripture you'll be studying. Cut out the cards in the back and read over them as you move through your day. Ask the Holy Spirit to help you commit these short verses to memory, and you will be encouraged by the truths written on your heart for the rest of your life!

Scripture:
We have included the portions of Scripture that you'll be studying in the workbook itself. Having the passage right in front of you will help with continuity and focus. Of course context matters, so please open your Bible at any point along the way to get a bigger picture of the scene.

Questions:
Rather than days, *The Amazing Life of Jesus Christ* is divided into studies. Depending on the content, some weeks will be longer than others, so you may need to adjust your time accordingly. There are five studies each week, and each contains an introduction, questions about the passage, and questions for personal application.

- Before you begin each study, pray and ask the Holy Spirit to open your eyes to see Jesus as never before. Pray for insights into His life and ministry. Pray for understanding and a teachable spirit. Pray that you would love Jesus more each day as you grow in your knowledge and understanding of Him and His mission on earth.

- Read completely through the blocked passage of Scripture before answering the questions.
- The first grouping of questions are about the passage itself and will encourage you to prayerfully think and observe truths from God's Word.
- Each section will have an **Application** question that will help you apply the truths of the passage to your own life.
- Sometimes, you'll discover a section titled **A Deeper Look**. This portion is optional, but will lead you into a deeper investigation of a specific truth seen in God's Word.

Wrapping Up:

This section is a simple summary of the theme, ideas, and truths from the week. As you read through these and digest what you've learned, stop and thank God for the ways He's revealed more of Himself and His Son to you each day, through His Word and by His Spirit.

ACKNOWLEDGEMENTS

The Amazing Life of Jesus Christ is based on the outstanding scholarly works of those who, through the centuries, have endeavored to put the life of Jesus Christ in chronological order. Using excerpts from the four Gospels, the events are placed during the time they most likely occurred. Although it is difficult to be absolutely certain of the following order of events, what *is* certain is that each event took place.

We are indebted to those who have done the hard work of placing the events in order, such as John MacArthur, Robert L. Thomas, Stanley N. Gundry, Johnston M. Cheney and others. Dr. Dwight Pentecost's and Dr. Oswald Sanders' works on Jesus were tremendously helpful as well.

A very special note of appreciation to the Lockman Foundation for giving us permission to use Scripture from the New American Standard Version and to B&H Publishing Group for the use of the maps taken from The Holman Bible Atlas.

I first met Leslie Strader several years ago at a leadership conference given by Dallas Theological Seminary. I was immediately impressed with her knowledge of Scripture and her joy for life. Years later, I invited her to come to a planning retreat with the board of Big Dream Ministries. This time I was impressed with her creativity and insights. When I found out she was a writer for a ministry magazine, I knew right away I wanted her to author the workbook for *The Amazing Life of Jesus Christ*. I will be forever grateful for that chance meeting in Dallas, and so appreciate her willingness to work with us on this study. Leslie is the wife of Ross, senior pastor of Bethel Bible Church, a thriving church in Tyler, Texas, and the mother of three children.

Pat Harley
President
Big Dream Ministries

JESUS, THE PREEXISTENT CREATOR

*"In the beginning was the Word, and the Word
was with God, and the Word was God."*
JOHN 1:1

The idea of preexistence can be a difficult concept. "Forever" is easier to envision in a future sense than looking "forever" into the past. Maybe it's because, although mankind hasn't always existed, man will live eternally. Man and woman were created in the image of God, but are still starkly different from Him, and this is one of the most distinct ways: there will not be an end to man's existence because human beings are created to live eternally; however, every human being had a beginning.

Jesus enters history in Luke 2 when, as John writes, "the Word became flesh" to dwell among us. But Paul says Jesus existed *before all things* (Colossians 1:17) — before time started ticking and space was filled and nothing was fashioned into everything. How challenging for limited, finite creatures to understand a limitless, infinite God!

The careful reader can see Christ throughout Scripture, and that inspired observation is faith building. In his book, *The Incomparable Christ*, J. Oswald Sanders says Christ's preexistence "is the foundation on which the whole superstructure of the Christian faith rests. If He was not preexistent, He cannot be God, and if He is not God, He cannot be Creator and Redeemer."

Today is the first step in a journey to know Jesus more intimately and love Him more deeply. This particular week is unique in our study. Before studying the life of Jesus, it is crucial to understand Him as the Preexistent Creator and why He needed to enter life on earth as our Rescuer and Redeemer.

Whether this is a brand-new thought or a well-traveled trail of meditation and study, pray for a bigger, grander view of Jesus as the infinite glory and image of God. Pray for a heart to treasure Him as the ever-existing Joy-Giver.

 **STUDY ONE
Joy in the Lord and Creation**

While the story of Jesus living on earth as a perfect Man begins in the Gospels, the story of God's intention to use His Son to draw us to Himself begins long before that — in eternity past, before a creating word was ever spoken. Jesus' birth, life, and death were never a "clean-up operation," set in motion when everything else fell through. It is for joy that God created us, saved us, and sustains an intimate relationship with us.

Psalms 16:11
"You will make known to me the path of life; in Your presence is fullness of joy; in Your right hand there are pleasures forever."

1. What is found and promised in this verse about the triune God (Father, Son, and Holy Spirit) and His desires toward us?

2. How should this shape your view of Christ as we journey through the gospels?

Isaiah 43:6b–7
"Bring My sons from afar, and My daughters from the ends of the earth, Everyone who is called by my name, And whom I have created for My glory, Whom I have formed, even whom I have made."

Job 38:6b–7
"Who laid its (the earth's) cornerstone, when the morning stars sang together and all the sons of God shouted for joy?"

Proverbs 8:30–31
"Then I (wisdom) was beside Him, as a master workman; And I was daily His delight, rejoicing always before Him, rejoicing in the world, His earth, And having my delight in the sons of men."

3. In what ways do you see God as the Giver of joy in these passages?

4. Why did God create man? What does it mean "He created him for His glory?"

5. In these verses, how do you see man as the pinnacle of God's creation, bringing glory to God?

Application

Describe what it means to be called by God's name (Isaiah 43:1-7). What is your response to a God who creates out of *joy*?

STUDY TWO
Jesus Who Existed Before Time, Space, and Matter

"Jesus was unique among men in that His birth did not mark His origin, but only His appearance as a man on the stage of time. . . . He did not become God's Son at the incarnation, or when He rose from the dead. He is God, supreme and without beginning."

J. Oswald Sanders, *The Incomparable Christ*

John 1:1–18

"In the beginning was the Word, and the Word was with God, and the Word was God. ² He was in the beginning with God. ³ All things came into being through Him, and apart from Him nothing came into being that has come into being. ⁴ In Him was life, and the life was the Light of men. ⁵ The Light shines in the darkness, and the darkness did not comprehend it. ⁶ There came a man sent from God, whose name was John. ⁷ He came as a witness to testify about the Light, so that all might believe through him. ⁸ He was not the Light, but he came to testify about the Light.

⁹ There was the true Light which, coming into the world, enlightens every man. ¹⁰ He was in the world, and the world was made through Him, and the world did not know Him. ¹¹ He came to His own, and those who were His own did not receive Him. ¹² But as many as received Him, to them He gave the right to become children of God, even to those who believe in His name, ¹³ who were born, not of blood nor of the will of the flesh nor of the will of man, but of God. ¹⁴ And the Word became flesh, and dwelt among us, and we saw His glory, glory as of the only begotten from the Father, full of grace and truth. ¹⁵ John testified about Him and cried out, saying, 'This was He of whom I said, 'He who comes after me has a higher rank than I, for He existed before me.' ¹⁶ For of His fullness we have all received, and grace upon grace. ¹⁷ For the Law was given through Moses; grace and truth were realized through Jesus Christ. ¹⁸ No one has seen God at any time; the only begotten God who is in the bosom of the Father, He has explained Him."

Colossians 1:15–18

"¹⁵ He is the image of the invisible God, the firstborn of all creation. ¹⁶ For by Him all things were created, both in the heavens and on earth, visible and invisible, whether thrones or dominions or rulers or authorities—all things have been created through Him and for Him. ¹⁷ He is before all things, and in Him all things hold together. ¹⁸ He is also head of the body, the church; and He is the beginning, the firstborn from the dead, so that He Himself will come to have first place in everything."

1 Corinthians 8:6
". . . yet for us there is but one God, the Father, from whom are all things and we exist for Him; and one Lord, Jesus Christ, by whom are all things, and we exist through Him."

1. Observe and record all the examples of preexistent language in these passages.

2. How does the author John describe Jesus' role in creation?

3. What does John 1:1–2 say Jesus did before creation? What does John 1:14,16–18 say Jesus did after creation? What was the effect on us?

4. What is the function of light? Why would John use "light" to describe Jesus? Who did the Light come to "enlighten?" (v. 9)

5. What do you see in this passage that describes the action God takes toward us? How is Jesus involved?

6. How does Paul describe Jesus in Colossians 1:15–18? From these passages, what do you see was Jesus' role in creation?

The word "firstborn" in the Greek is *prototokos*, a term referring to priority in time or rank. Much like the heir of a king, Jesus is supreme in His status and possesses all the privileges and rights over creation as God Himself. Paul is not saying Jesus was created (an Arian heresy), and that is clear from the context as well.

7. In 1 Corinthians 8:6, what does Paul say is Jesus' role in the world? What is our role in our relationship with Him?

Application

Why is it important to your faith that Jesus is preexistent, present at creation with God the Father and God the Spirit?

A DEEPER LOOK

Read the passages below. Write down your observations about Jesus: Who is He? What attributes do you see? What does He do?

Ephesians 1:1-23   Colossians 1:15-23   Hebrews 1:1-4

STUDY THREE
Rebellion: Man's Joy Lost

You may ask, "Why are we going back to Genesis 3 in the Old Testament when we are studying the life of Christ in the New Testament?" It is in this chapter that the great separation between God and man began. It explains what is man's problem and why Jesus had to come to earth, live a perfect life, and die for the sins of man. It is crucial to understanding the gospel message.

Genesis 3:1–22

"Now the serpent was more crafty than any beast of the field which the Lord God had made. And he said to the woman, 'Indeed, has God said, 'You shall not eat from any tree of the garden'?' **2** The woman said to the serpent, 'From the fruit of the trees of the garden we may eat; **3** but from the fruit of the tree which is in the middle of the garden, God has said, 'You shall not eat from it or touch it, or you will die.' **4** The serpent said to the woman, 'You surely will not die! **5** For God knows that in the day you eat from it your eyes will be opened, and you will be like God, knowing good and evil.' **6** When the woman saw that the tree was good for food, and that it was a delight to the eyes, and that the tree was desirable to make one wise, she took from its fruit and ate; and she gave also to her husband with her, and he ate. **7** Then the eyes of both of them were opened, and they knew that they were naked; and they sewed fig leaves together and made themselves loin coverings.

8 They heard the sound of the Lord God walking in the garden in the cool of the day, and the man and his wife hid themselves from the presence of the Lord God among the trees of the garden. **9** Then the Lord God called to the man, and said to him, 'Where are you?' **10** He said, 'I heard the sound of You in the garden, and I was afraid because I was naked; so I hid myself.' **11** And He said, 'Who told you that you were naked? Have you eaten from the tree of which I commanded you not to eat?' **12** The man said, 'The woman whom You gave to be with me, she gave me from the tree, and I ate.' **13** Then the Lord God said to the woman, 'What is this you have done?' And the woman said, 'The serpent deceived me, and I ate.'

14 The Lord God said to the serpent,
'Because you have done this,
Cursed are you more than all cattle,
And more than every beast of the field;
On your belly you will go,
And dust you will eat
All the days of your life;
15 And I will put enmity
Between you and the woman,
And between your seed and her seed;
He shall bruise you on the head,
And you shall bruise him on the heel.'
16 To the woman He said,
'I will greatly multiply
Your pain in childbirth,
In pain you will bring forth children;
Yet your desire will be for your husband,
And he will rule over you.'
17 Then to Adam He said, "Because you have listened to the voice of your wife, and have eaten from the tree about which I commanded you, saying, 'You shall not eat from it;'
Cursed is the ground because of you;
In toil you will eat of it
All the days of your life.
18 'Both thorns and thistles it shall grow for you;
And you will eat the plants of the field;
19 By the sweat of your face
You will eat bread,
Till you return to the ground,
Because from it you were taken;
For you are dust,
And to dust you shall return.'

20 Now the man called his wife's name Eve, because she was the mother of all the living. **21** The Lord God made garments of skin for Adam and his wife, and clothed them.

22 Then the Lord God said, 'Behold, the man has become like one of Us, knowing good and evil; and now, he might stretch out his hand, and take also from the tree of life, and eat, and live forever" — **23** therefore the Lord God sent him out from the garden of Eden, to cultivate the ground from which he was taken. **24** So He drove the man out; and at the east of the garden of Eden He stationed the cherubim and the flaming sword which turned every direction to guard the way to the tree of life."

 NOTE: When Scripture talks about God, it is God in three persons: Father, Son, and Holy Spirit.

1. How do these passages describe Satan?

2. Compare what Satan said in verse 1 and what Eve said in verses 3–4 to what God said in Genesis 2:15–17. What is different and how does that matter?

3. Write down evidences of sin mentioned or implied.

 NOTE: Sin is rebellion against God and/or a transgression of His law.

4. What was Adam and Eve's sin?

5. What does it mean when Scripture says, "the eyes of both of them were opened?"

6. God entered this scandalous scene in Genesis 3:8 and began asking questions. Write down the questions He asked. Why would an all-knowing, omniscient God ask questions?

7. List the judgments the Lord God pronounces on the characters below. Pay special attention to what was cursed:

   a. the serpent

   b. Eve

   c. Adam

8. How do those judgments still affect the world and relationships today?

9. What does Scripture say about why the LORD God banished Adam and Eve from the Garden?

10. Where is Jesus in this scene? Where is the Trinity in this scene?

11. Grace is unmerited favor. How is the grace of God shown in the garden scene?

Application
How are your eyes "opened" to sin in your life? What keeps you from seeing it? See Psalms 32:3–5, John 16:7–8, Hebrews 4:12, and James 4:17 for insight.

What does Scripture say are some of the reasons we sin?

Judges 21:25   Romans 1:18–32

Psalms 52:3   Titus 3:3

 STUDY FOUR
The Consequences of Sin

God said, "If you eat this fruit you will surely die." The commandment was clear and precise. Adam and Eve's choice to disobey was an act of unjustified, open, horrific, and absolute rebellion against the very One who had created everything in joy and given them everything in the world for their pleasure—except the fruit of one tree. The results were more than they could have ever anticipated.

Romans 3:10–12
"10 . . . as it is written, 'There is none righteous, not even one; 11 There is none who understands, there is none who seeks for God; 12 all have turned aside, together they have become useless; there is none who does good, there is not even one.'"

Romans 1:18–21
"18 For the wrath of God is revealed from heaven against all ungodliness and unrighteousness of men who suppress the truth in unrighteousness, 19 because that which is known about God is evident within them; for God made it evident to them. 20 For since the creation of the world His invisible attributes, His eternal power and divine nature, have been clearly seen, being understood through what has been made, so that they are without excuse. 21 For even though they knew God, they did not honor Him as God or give thanks, but they became futile in their speculations, and their foolish heart was darkened."

1. What does Romans 3:10–12 say is the natural condition of all mankind?

2. What is man's posture toward God apart from Christ? What is God's relationship with man like apart from Christ?

3. What does Paul in Romans 1:21 say men neglected to do? What affect did that have on them?

Application

Adam and Eve were tempted by the serpent in the Garden. What is temptation? Is temptation sin? Why or why not? (James 1:14–15) What does God's Word say you can do to guard against falling into temptation? What does God say He will do for you? (see 1 Peter 5:6-11, Ephesians 6:10–17, James 4:6–10.)

A DEEPER LOOK

Read Genesis 6:5, Psalms 51:5, Isaiah 64:6, Jeremiah 17:9, Romans 3:23, Ephesians 2:1–4.

Summarize what God's Word declares about the natural state of man. Based on Scripture, do you think mankind is inherently good or bad? How does this influence your thinking about yourself and mankind's need for a Savior?

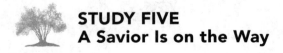

STUDY FIVE
A Savior Is on the Way

Man was helplessly lost in his sin, eternally separated from God and deserving only His wrath. Yet in His grace, God raised up writing prophets to give hope to His children and assurance that He had not abandoned them, but was going to send someone to save them from their sins. Numerous prophecies in the Old Testament pointed the way and assured the people that help was coming and, with it, returned joy. A few of those prophecies follow.

Jeremiah 23:5–6

"⁵ 'Behold, the days are coming,' declares the Lord, 'When I will raise up for David a righteous Branch; And He will reign as king and act wisely And do justice and righteousness in the land. ⁶ 'In His days Judah will be saved, and Israel will dwell securely; And this is His name by which He will be called, 'The Lord our righteousness.'"

Isaiah 9:6-7

"⁶ For a child will be born to us, a son will be given to us; And the government will rest on His shoulders; And His name will be called Wonderful Counselor, Mighty God, Eternal Father, Prince of Peace. ⁷ There will be no end to the increase of His government or of peace, on the throne of David and over his kingdom, To establish it and to uphold it with justice and righteousness From then on and forevermore. The zeal of the Lord of hosts will accomplish this."

Micah 5:2

"But as for you Bethlehem Ephrathah, Too little to be among the clans of Judah, from you One will go forth for Me to be ruler in Israel. His goings forth are from long ago, From the days of eternity."

Zechariah 9:9–10

"Rejoice greatly daughter of Zion! Shout in triumph daughter of Jerusalem! Behold your king is coming to you; He is just and endowed with salvation, Humble, and mounted on a donkey, Even on a colt, the foal of a donkey . . . He will speak peace to the nations; and His dominion will be from sea to sea, and from the River to the ends of the earth."

 NOTE: The prophets Isaiah and Micah wrote about 700 years before Jesus was born; Jeremiah 600 years, and Zechariah 500 years before the coming of Christ to earth.

1. What are the promised prophecies spoken in Jeremiah and Isaiah? How have they been fulfilled?

2. Observe and record here what is known about Jesus from the prophet Isaiah.

3. What is known about Jesus from the prophet Jeremiah?

4. What does Zechariah promise will be seen in and done by Jesus?

5. What hint does Micah give about Jesus coming?

6. According to Zechariah, what is to be our response to our King, Jesus?

Application

Read Romans 3:23–26. What does Paul say is our natural spiritual condition in verse 23? What gift has God provided to address that need? How is that gift received? What is your response to His offer?

A DEEPER LOOK

Read Psalms 95:1. Make a list of ten things you are thankful for and pray it as praise to God. Stretch yourself! Write a hymn or poem of praise to God, the One who prophets said would come to save mankind.

WRAPPING UP

This week, Scripture demonstrated Jesus as existing eternally, creating joyfully, and rescuing perfectly. God's Truth has also shined its light on our state of rebellion, depravity, and desperate need. There is only one response to a God who shows His great love for us by sending His only Son — worship!

~ Map of Jesus' Childhood ~

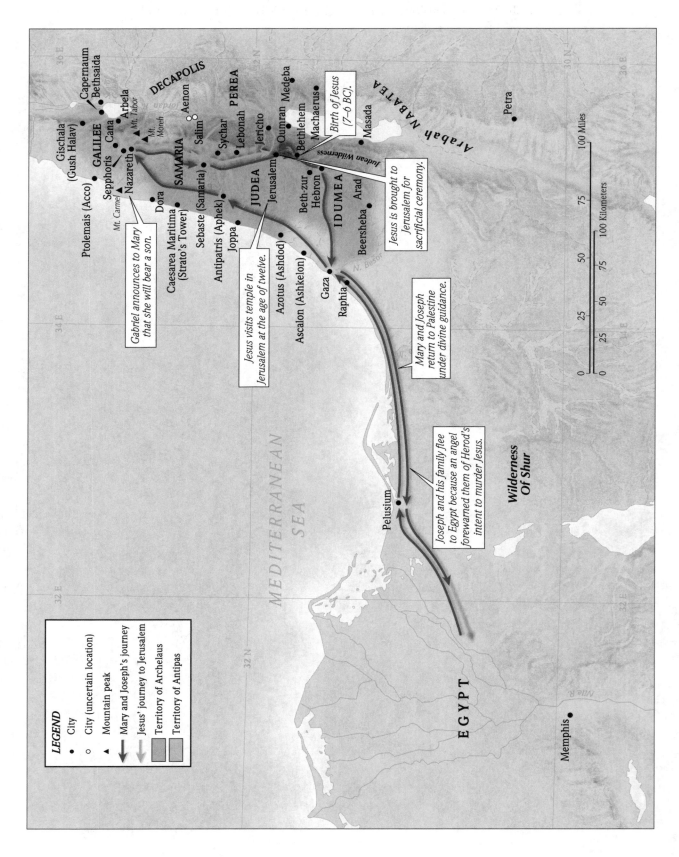

Capernaum
Bethsaida
DECAPOLIS
Arbela
Mt. Tabor
Cana
PEREA
Aenon
Medeba
Birth of Jesus (7–6 BC).
Petra
Gischala (Gush Halav)
GALILEE
Mt. Moreh
Salim
Sychar
Lebonah
Qumran
Bethlehem
Machaerus
Sepphoris
SAMARIA
Jericho
Ptolemais (Acco)
Nazareth
Judean Wilderness
Masada
Arabah NABATEA
Mt. Carmel
Dora
JUDEA
Jerusalem
Jesus is brought to Jerusalem for sacrificial ceremony.
Caesarea Maritima (Strato's Tower)
Sebaste (Samaria)
Beth-zur
Hebron
IDUMEA
Arad
Gabriel announces to Mary that she will bear a son.
Antipatris (Aphek)
Joppa
Beersheba
Jesus visits temple in Jerusalem at the age of twelve.
Azotus (Ashdod)
Ascalon (Ashkelon)
Gaza
N. Besor
Raphia
Mary and Joseph return to Palestine under divine guidance.

100 Miles
100 Kilometers
75
50
75
25
50
50
25
0
0

MEDITERRANEAN SEA

Joseph and his family flee to Egypt because an angel forewarned them of Herod's intent to murder Jesus.

Pelusium

Wilderness Of Shur

EGYPT

Nile R.

Memphis

LEGEND
• City
○ City (uncertain location)
▲ Mountain peak
↓ Mary and Joseph's journey
↓ Jesus' journey to Jerusalem
  Territory of Archelaus
  Territory of Antipas

JESUS, GOD-SENT

"He will be great and will be called the Son of the Most High; and the Lord God will give Him the throne of His father David; and He will reign over the house of Jacob forever, and His kingdom will have no end."
LUKE 1:32–33

The birth of Jesus is a favorite of songwriters and storytellers. A silent, dark night. A few bleating sheep. And then suddenly—the sky explodes! Darkness is displaced by the magnificence of heaven. Ragged men fall on their knees and tremble like leaves in the wind. Their ears and hearts hear that the long wait is over.

This is the space in time decreed before the foundations of the earth were laid that Jesus would enter humanity as our Deliverer and Redeemer. And God the Father is using each character in this sacred story to bring Him glory. Man sees a poor Jewish girl, in over her head. God sees a vessel, willing to be poured out for magnificent, eternal purposes. Man sees dirty sheepherders, the lower class of the day, hanging out on a hillside. God sees the caretakers of His kingdom, humble men trusted to spread the news that the Messiah had arrived. Man sees a hole in the wall in a backwater town. God sees the perfect place to host the most holy event in history, the birth of Jesus.

In the passages today, the glory of the Lord in the person of Jesus is being revealed to all flesh. Innkeepers and Angels. Wise men and Shepherds. Every tribe and people and nation and tongue. To every creature in heaven and on earth and under the earth and in the sea . . . and to us!

Prayerfully read, study, and meditate on these passages that tell the story of our Savior's birth. Ask the Lord to help you behold His Son with fresh eyes and an open heart.

STUDY ONE
The Genealogy of Jesus

"What is this doing here?"

That—or something like it—is often the first thought that comes to mind when a long, monotonous list of names appears in the Bible. Most people usually skim or totally skip over them. But there's a good reason not to: "*All Scripture is inspired by God and profitable for teaching, for reproof, for correction, for training in righteousness . . .*" (2 Timothy 3:16)

Because God's Word testifies truthfully about itself, it is certain that "*. . . whatever was written in earlier times was written for our instruction, so that through perseverance and the encouragement of the*

Scriptures we might have hope." (Romans 15:4) That includes genealogies!

Let's prove this out by taking a closer look at some of these names in the lineage of Christ—specifically, the women. What do we learn about ourselves and our Lord from this list of names and the stories behind them? And how can it bring joy?

Matthew 1:1–17

"The record of the genealogy of Jesus the Messiah, the son of David, the son of Abraham:

2 Abraham was the father of Isaac, Isaac the father of Jacob, and Jacob the father of Judah and his brothers. **3** Judah was the father of Perez and Zerah by Tamar, Perez was the father of Hezron, and Hezron the father of Ram. **4** Ram was the father of Amminadab, Amminadab the father of Nahshon, and Nahshon the father of Salmon. **5** Salmon was the father of Boaz by Rahab, Boaz was the father of Obed by Ruth, and Obed the father of Jesse. **6** Jesse was the father of David the king.

David was the father of Solomon by Bathsheba who had been the wife of Uriah. **7** Solomon was the father of Rehoboam, Rehoboam the father of Abijah, and Abijah the father of Asa. **8** Asa was the father of Jehoshaphat, Jehoshaphat the father of Joram, and Joram the father of Uzziah. **9** Uzziah was the father of Jotham, Jotham the father of Ahaz, and Ahaz the father of Hezekiah. **10** Hezekiah was the father of Manasseh, Manasseh the father of Amon, and Amon the father of Josiah. **11** Josiah became the father of Jeconiah and his brothers, at the time of the deportation to Babylon.

12 After the deportation to Babylon: Jeconiah became the father of Shealtiel, and Shealtiel the father of Zerubbabel. **13** Zerubbabel was the father of Abihud, Abihud the father of Eliakim, and Eliakim the father of Azor. **14** Azor was the father of Zadok, Zadok the father of Achim, and Achim the father of Eliud. **15** Eliud was the father of Eleazar, Eleazar the father of Matthan, and Matthan the father of Jacob. **16** Jacob was the father of Joseph the husband of Mary, by whom Jesus was born, who is called the Messiah. **17** So all the generations from Abraham to David are fourteen generations; from David to the deportation to Babylon, fourteen generations; and from the deportation to Babylon to the Messiah, fourteen generations."

Luke 3:23–38

"**23** When He began His ministry, Jesus Himself was about thirty years of age, being, as was supposed, the son of Joseph, the son of Eli, **24** the son of Matthat, the son of Levi, the son of Melchi, the son of Jannai, the son of Joseph, **25** the son of Mattathias, the son of Amos, the son of Nahum, the son of Hesli, the son of Naggai, **26** the son of Maath, the son of Mattathias, the son of Semein, the son of Josech, the son of Joda, **27** the son of Joanan, the son of Rhesa, the son of Zerubbabel, the son of Shealtiel, the son of Neri, **28** the son of Melchi, the son of Addi, the son of Cosam, the son of Elmadam, the son of Er, **29** the son of Joshua, the son of Eliezer, the son of Jorim, the son of Matthat, the son of Levi, **30** the son of Simeon, the son of Judah, the son of Joseph, the son of Jonam, the son of Eliakim, **31** the son of Melea, the son of Menna, the son of Mattatha, the son of Nathan, the son of David, **32** the son of Jesse, the son of Obed, the son of Boaz, the son of Salmon, the son of Nahshon, **33** the son of Amminadab, the son of

Admin, the son of Ram, the son of Hezron, the son of Perez, the son of Judah, **34** the son of Jacob, the son of Isaac, the son of Abraham, the son of Terah, the son of Nahor, **35** the son of Serug, the son of Reu, the son of Peleg, the son of Heber, the son of Shelah, **36** the son of Cainan, the son of Arphaxad, the son of Shem, the son of Noah, the son of Lamech, **37** the son of Methuselah, the son of Enoch, the son of Jared, the son of Mahalaleel, the son of Cainan, **38** the son of Enosh, the son of Seth, the son of Adam, the son of God."

Matthew 1:3 — TAMAR. Read Genesis 38:1–30, a passage that feels almost like an interruption in the story of Joseph. Based on the background provided in Genesis 38, what do you learn about Tamar? What was her relationship with Judah? Record your observations.

Matthew 1:5 — RAHAB. Read Joshua 2 and 6:22–25. Who is Rahab? How was she used by God in the life of Israel? *Rahab's son Boaz became the husband of Ruth.*

Matthew 1:5 — RUTH. Read Ruth 1 to discover Ruth's origins and to read of her commitment. Write any observations below. How does this story end? (Ruth 4:13–22) *Ruth's son Obed became the grandfather of King David.*

Matthew 1:6 — BATHSHEBA. Read 2 Samuel 11 and record any observations about "the wife of Uriah."

1. A quick read of 2 Kings will reveal that most every other name in the lists recorded by Matthew and Luke is descended from royalty. What does the inclusion of four women in the genealogy of Christ say to us about His character?

2. Scandal in some form or fashion is connected to each of the four women listed here. What does the inclusion of these women in the genealogy of Christ communicate about His relationship with sinners or those far from Him?

3. How do these genealogies affirm God's promises to His people and God's love for the whole world into which He sent His Son?

4. Compare Matthew's and Luke's genealogies. What is different about them? How do they support each other?

STUDY TWO
Prophesies and Promises

The accounts of Gabriel delivering birth announcements to Zacharias and Mary share many parallels. The families were connected by blood, both births seemed impossible in every way, and the purpose of each child's life was known to his parents before either drew his first breath on earth. Into humble circumstances came an unexpected high calling. Yet with all the similarities, there is a record of differing responses that is instructive to us. "Fear not, have faith," the angel said, and only one obeyed. And yet, Immanuel came and the way was prepared. And nothing has ever been the same.

Luke 1:1–25

"Inasmuch as many have undertaken to compile an account of the things accomplished among us, ² just as they were handed down to us by those who from the beginning were eyewitnesses and servants of the word, ³ it seemed fitting for me as well, having investigated everything carefully from the beginning, to write it out for you in consecutive order, most excellent Theophilus; ⁴ so that you may know the exact truth about the things you have been taught.

⁵ In the days of Herod, king of Judea, there was a priest named Zacharias, of the division of Abijah; and he had a wife from the daughters of Aaron, and her name was Elizabeth. ⁶ They were both righteous in the sight of God, walking blamelessly in all the commandments and requirements of the Lord. ⁷ But they had no child, because Elizabeth was barren, and they were both advanced in years.

⁸ Now it happened that while he was performing his priestly service before God in the appointed order of his division, ⁹ according to the custom of the priestly office, he was chosen by lot to enter the temple of the Lord and burn incense. ¹⁰ And the whole multitude of the people were in prayer outside at the hour of the incense offering. ¹¹ And an angel of the Lord appeared to him, standing to the right of the altar of incense. ¹² Zacharias was troubled when he saw the angel, and fear gripped him. ¹³ But the angel said to him, 'Do not be afraid, Zacharias,

for your petition has been heard, and your wife Elizabeth will bear you a son, and you will give him the name John. **14** You will have joy and gladness, and many will rejoice at his birth. **15** For he will be great in the sight of the Lord; and he will drink no wine or liquor, and he will be filled with the Holy Spirit while yet in his mother's womb. **16** And he will turn many of the sons of Israel back to the Lord their God. **17** It is he who will go as a forerunner before Him in the spirit and power of Elijah, to turn the hearts of the fathers back to the children, and the disobedient to the attitude of the righteous, so as to make ready a people prepared for the Lord.'

18 Zacharias said to the angel, 'How will I know this for certain? For I am an old man and my wife is advanced in years.' **19** The angel answered and said to him, 'I am Gabriel, who stands in the presence of God, and I have been sent to speak to you and to bring you this good news. **20** And behold, you shall be silent and unable to speak until the day when these things take place, because you did not believe my words, which will be fulfilled in their proper time.'

21 The people were waiting for Zacharias, and were wondering at his delay in the temple. **22** But when he came out, he was unable to speak to them; and they realized that he had seen a vision in the temple; and he kept making signs to them, and remained mute. **23** When the days of his priestly service were ended, he went back home.

24 After these days Elizabeth his wife became pregnant, and she kept herself in seclusion for five months, saying, **25** 'This is the way the Lord has dealt with me in the days when He looked with favor upon me, to take away my disgrace among men.'"

1. Record biographical information about Zacharias and Elizabeth contained in verses 5–7. (Zacharias means "the LORD remembers"; Elizabeth means "oath of God.") What had Zacharias been chosen to do in verse 8–9? (see Exodus 30:7–8)

NOTE:

1 Chronicles 24 explains how David divided the priests into divisions, with verse 19 connecting directly to Luke 1:8–9. Scholars say this was a special privilege for Zacharias because selection was almost impossible in terms of the odds—there were somewhere between 18,000–24,000 potential candidate priests available for this work; if chosen, it was once in a lifetime.

2. Define *sovereignty*. (use www.biblestudytools.com) How do verses 8–9 reflect the sovereignty of God? (see Proverbs 16:33)

3. What was Zacharias' response to the angel's appearance (v. 12)?

4. Read verses 13–17.
   • What comfort did Gabriel give to Zacharias?

   • What was John's "job description" according to Gabriel?

   • What is Zacharias told would be the response to the birth of John?

5. How did the old priest receive the angel's message? How did Gabriel respond and what was the consequence? (vv. 18–20) How do we see God's mercy in this scene?

6. How did Elizabeth experience and respond to the work of God in her life? (vv. 24–25)

Application
Zacharias experienced a consequence for unbelief. What consequences have you experienced for a lack of faith? What impact did it have immediately? Long-term?

MARY AND THE ANGEL GABRIEL IN NAZARETH

Luke 1:26–56
"26 Now in the sixth month the angel Gabriel was sent from God to a city in Galilee called Nazareth, 27 to a virgin engaged to a man whose name was Joseph, of the descendants of David; and the virgin's name was Mary. 28 And coming in, he said to her, "Greetings, favored one! The Lord is with you." 29 But she was very perplexed at this statement, and kept pondering what kind of salutation this was. 30 The angel said to her, 'Do not be afraid, Mary; for you have found favor with God. 31 And behold, you will conceive in your womb and bear a son, and you shall name Him Jesus. 32 He will be great and will be called the Son of the Most High; and the Lord God will give Him the throne of His father David; 33 and He will reign over the house of Jacob forever, and His kingdom will have no end.'

34 Mary said to the angel, 'How can this be, since I am a virgin?' **35** The angel answered and said to her, 'The Holy Spirit will come upon you, and the power of the Most High will overshadow you; and for that reason the holy Child shall be called the Son of God. **36** And behold, even your relative Elizabeth has also conceived a son in her old age; and she who was called barren is now in her sixth month. **37** For nothing will be impossible with God.' **38** And Mary said, 'Behold, the bondslave of the Lord; may it be done to me according to your word.' And the angel departed from her.

39 Now at this time Mary arose and went in a hurry to the hill country, to a city of Judah, **40** and entered the house of Zacharias and greeted Elizabeth. **41** When Elizabeth heard Mary's greeting, the baby leaped in her womb; and Elizabeth was filled with the Holy Spirit. **42** And she cried out with a loud voice and said, 'Blessed are you among women, and blessed is the fruit of your womb! **43** And how has it happened to me, that the mother of my Lord would come to me? **44** For behold, when the sound of your greeting reached my ears, the baby leaped in my womb for joy. **45** And blessed is she who believed that there would be a fulfillment of what had been spoken to her by the Lord."

46 And Mary said: "My soul exalts the Lord,
47 And my spirit has rejoiced in God my Savior.
48 'For He has had regard for the humble state of His bondslave;
For behold, from this time on all generations will count me blessed.
49 'For the Mighty One has done great things for me;
And holy is His name.
50 'And His mercy is upon generation after generation
Toward those who fear Him.
51 'He has done mighty deeds with His arm;
He has scattered those who were proud in the thoughts of their heart.
52 'He has brought down rulers from their thrones,
And has exalted those who were humble.
53 'He has filled the hungry with good things;
And sent away the rich empty-handed.
54 'He has given help to Israel His servant,
In remembrance of His mercy,
55 As He spoke to our fathers,
To Abraham and his descendants forever.'
56 And Mary stayed with her about three months, and then returned to her home."

1. Write down the geographical and biographical information given in verses 26–27. What does "the sixth month" refer to in this passage?

NOTE: In the culture of the Ancient Near East, "betrothed" meant "engaged," a legal arrangement considered as binding as marriage, but did not include a sexual relationship.

2. How did Gabriel greet Mary? Read Mary's response in verse 29. Why would this greeting "perplex" her?

3. What was Gabriel's first command to Mary (v. 30)? What do we learn about Jesus from the angel? (vv. 31–33)?

4. What was the difference in Zacharias' and Mary's responses to the news of a birth in their family? How do we know they responded differently?

5. How did Gabriel build Mary's faith in his proclamation (v. 36)? How did Mary respond? (v. 38)

6. Gabriel foretold that John would be filled with the Holy Spirit even in his mother's womb (v. 15). This passage describes Elizabeth as being filled with the Holy Spirit (v. 41). What prompted that "filling?" And what did the Spirit enable her (and the baby in her womb) to do?

7. Due to his lack of faith, Zacharias was unable to utter one word after he received the news he'd been longing to hear all his life. In contrast, Mary humbly sang a hymn of praise. Her song is called "The Magnificat," Latin for *magnify*. Who is the subject of Mary's song? What does the song say God does? What does the song say Mary does?

Application

When the angel appeared to Mary with his heavenly message, she must have experienced a wide range of emotions. Put yourself in her place and write a few sentences about what that moment might have been like.

Then, write your own "Magnificat" modeled after Mary. Praise Him for who He is in your life and all He has done!

A DEEPER LOOK

Read these verses and write down anything new or encouraging you learn about the Holy Spirit who indwells believers.

Romans 5:5   Ephesians 1:11–14

Romans 8:26–27   Ephesians 3:14–21

Galatians 4:6   Titus 3:5–6

STUDY THREE
Zacharias and Joseph: Preparing the Way

This week, we look at Zacharias and Joseph, two men who needed help in their unbelief. And who could blame them? A barren old woman and a teenage virgin, both giving birth? That's not something you see every day! And so, because they were blinded by their fears, God graciously and generously allowed them to see. One through a time of testing and correction; the other, in a dream. Their submitted hearts settled peacefully with the unknown and that led them to worship and obedience.

Luke 1:57–80
"**57** Now the time had come for Elizabeth to give birth, and she gave birth to a son. 58 Her neighbors and her relatives heard that the Lord had displayed His great mercy toward her; and they were rejoicing with her.
59 And it happened that on the eighth day they came to circumcise the child, and they were going to call him Zacharias, after his father. **60** But his mother answered and said, 'No indeed; but he shall be called John.' **61** And they said to her, 'There is no one among your relatives who is called by that name.' **62** And they made signs to his father, as to what he wanted him called. **63** And he asked for a tablet and wrote as follows, 'His name is John.' And they were all astonished. 64 And

at once his mouth was opened and his tongue loosed, and he began to speak in praise of God. **65** Fear came on all those living around them; and all these matters were being talked about in all the hill country of Judea. **66** All who heard them kept them in mind, saying, "What then will this child turn out to be?" For the hand of the Lord was certainly with him.

67 And his father Zacharias was filled with the Holy Spirit, and prophesied, saying:

68 'Blessed be the Lord God of Israel,

For He has visited us and accomplished redemption for His people,

69 And has raised up a horn of salvation for us

In the house of David His servant —

70 As He spoke by the mouth of His holy prophets from of old —

71 Salvation from our enemies,

And from the hand of all who hate us;

72 To show mercy toward our fathers,

And to remember His holy covenant,

73 The oath which He swore to Abraham our father,

74 To grant us that we, being rescued from the hand of our enemies,

Might serve Him without fear,

75 In holiness and righteousness before Him all our days.

76 'And you, child, will be called the prophet of the Most High;

For you will go on before the Lord to prepare His ways;

77 To give to His people the knowledge of salvation

By the forgiveness of their sins,

78 Because of the tender mercy of our God,

With which the Sunrise from on high will visit us,

79 To shine upon those who sit in darkness and the shadow of death,

To guide our feet into the way of peace.'

80 And the child continued to grow and to become strong in spirit, and he lived in the deserts until the day of his public appearance to Israel."

1. What was the response to the fulfilled prophecy of John's birth (v. 58)?

2. When was Zacharias able to speak again? What precipitated this? How did the people respond?

3. Why was it important for John to be named John?

The name "John" means "Yahweh is gracious" or "Gift of Yahweh."

4. What did Zacharias do after he was able to speak again? How did the people respond?

5. What does verse 67 say Zacharias did and how was he able to do this? How does Zacharias describe the role of Jesus (vv. 68–75)? How does he describe the role of John (vv. 76–77)? What will each accomplish for the people (vv. 77–79)?

6. What do we learn about John the Baptist from verse 80? From prophecy in Malachi 3:1?

Application

Look up the words "humble" and "humility" in the dictionary to get a clear understanding of what those words mean. Humility plays a crucial role for anyone called to serve God. Where do you see that in the lives of Zacharias and Elizabeth? Do you see evidence of humility in your life?

JOSEPH'S DREAM

Matthew 1:18–25

"**18** Now the birth of Jesus Christ was as follows: when His mother Mary had been betrothed to Joseph, before they came together she was found to be with child by the Holy Spirit. **19** And Joseph her husband, being a righteous man and not wanting to disgrace her, planned to send her away secretly. **20** But when he had considered this, behold, an angel of the Lord appeared to him in a dream, saying, 'Joseph, son of David, do not be afraid to take Mary as your wife; for the Child who has been conceived in her is of the Holy Spirit. **21** She will bear a Son; and you shall call His name Jesus, for He will save His people from their sins.' **22** Now all this took place to fulfill what was spoken by the Lord through the prophet: **23** 'Behold, the virgin shall be with child and shall bear a Son, and they shall call His name Immanuel,' which translated means, 'God with us.' **24** And Joseph awoke from his sleep and did as the angel of the Lord commanded him, and took Mary as his wife, **25** but kept her a virgin until she gave birth to a Son; and he called His name Jesus."

1. Mary was a virgin. How does Scripture say her pregnancy was accomplished (v. 20)?

2. These eight verses in Matthew 1 give more detail about Joseph — the earthly father of Jesus — than anywhere else in the Bible. It is also important to note there are no recorded words of Joseph in all of Scripture. Record any observations seen or implied about Joseph from this passage. What do these verses reveal about the character and the heart of Joseph? How is interaction with the angel different from Zacharias' or Mary's?

3. In the eyes of everyone around her, Mary was an adulterer. What was the punishment for adultery under the Law? See Deuteronomy 22:23–24.

4. How do the angel's words to Joseph about Jesus expand on what has already been revealed about the coming Son of God? (v. 21)

5. What attributes of God do you see at work or on display in this passage?

Application

God often asks men and women to trust Him and then obey, risking their comfort and reputation. Like Mary, have you ever been faced with that kind of sacrifice for following Jesus? Have you ever been afraid of doing something you know God has asked you to do? How did you respond?

STUDY FOUR
The Birth and Dedication of Jesus

Jesus — the Child who changed the world. The Lamb and the Lion. Wonderful. Counselor. Mighty God. Everlasting Father. Prince of Peace. The Beginning and End and Center and Subject of it all. He came to take away the sins of the world, and in a form we never imagined. But, there were those with eyes to see, and so they did at the appointed time. From shepherds on a hillside to servants in His temple, God, in His faithfulness, provided a chosen few with a great gift — a glimpse of the Way, the Truth, and the Life, bundled as a helpless baby. Redemption had arrived and the glory of the Lord was revealed!

Luke 2:1–20

"Now in those days a decree went out from Caesar Augustus, that a census be taken of all the inhabited earth. **2** This was the first census taken while Quirinius was governor of Syria. **3** And everyone was on his way to register for the census, each to his own city. **4** Joseph also went up from Galilee, from the city of Nazareth, to Judea, to the city of David which is called Bethlehem, because he was of the house and family of David, **5** in order to register along with Mary, who was engaged to him, and was with child. **6** While they were there, the days were completed for her to give birth. **7** And she gave birth to her firstborn son; and she wrapped Him in cloths, and laid Him in a manger, because there was no room for them in the inn.

8 In the same region there were some shepherds staying out in the fields and keeping watch over their flock by night. **9** And an angel of the Lord suddenly stood before them, and the glory of the Lord shone around them; and they were terribly frightened. **10** But the angel said to them, 'Do not be afraid; for behold, I bring you good news of great joy which will be for all the people; **11** for today in the city of David there has been born for you a Savior, who is Christ the Lord. **12** This will be a sign for you: you will find a baby wrapped in cloths and lying in a manger.' **13** And suddenly there appeared with the angel a multitude of the heavenly host praising God and saying,

14 "Glory to God in the highest,
And on earth peace among men with whom He is pleased."

15 When the angels had gone away from them into heaven, the shepherds began saying to one another, 'Let us go straight to Bethlehem then, and see this thing that has happened which the Lord has made known to us.' **16** So they came in a hurry and found their way to Mary and Joseph, and the baby as He lay in the manger. **17** When they had seen this, they made known the statement which had been told them about this Child. **18** And all who heard it wondered at the things which were told them by the shepherds. **19** But Mary treasured all these things, pondering them in her heart. **20** The shepherds went back, glorifying and praising God for all that they had heard and seen, just as had been told them."

1. How is God's sovereignty at work in verses 1–5? (see Micah 5:2; Jeremiah 14:8; Proverbs 21:1)

2. Verse 7 is the highest point in all of history thus far — the Messiah has arrived! Yet it is a very simple scene, recounted as "just the facts" with little detail, commentary, or emotion. The glory of this truth is seen in other parts of the Bible. Read Luke 1:67–79 again with this event in mind. Then read Isaiah 9:2, 6–7. What perspective do these verses give on the coming of Jesus to the simple account in Luke 2:7?

3. "Heavenly hosts" usually refers to an army of angels. What was the message of this "army" to the shepherds and the world (v. 14)? What might this experience have been like for the shepherds?

4. Underline the action words used in verses 17–20. What is the response of the shepherds to the Child? Of those who heard about His birth? What was Mary's response?

Application

The response to Jesus of the characters in this story (verses 17–20) are instructive to us. There are times to boldly proclaim who Jesus is to the world around us, and there are times to treasure and ponder who He is in our hearts. How are both equally important? Are you better at one than the other?

A DEEPER LOOK

Mary knew she was carrying the promised, long-anticipated Messiah, yet there is no record of her receiving "special treatment" for what the Lord had called her to do. What are examples of times and places Mary and Joseph could have been treated with more honor as the earthly parents of the Son of God?

Do we expect God to make things convenient for us or do we imagine that we are entitled to special favor when we are trying to follow His will? How is there joy in obedience, whatever the cost?

Read the following to answer that question:

John 16:33   James 1:2–4   2 Timothy 3:12

Philippians 1:29   1 Peter 4:12–19

JESUS IS DEDICATED IN JERUSALEM

Luke 2:21–38

"**21** And when eight days had passed, before His circumcision, His name was then called Jesus, the name given by the angel before He was conceived in the womb. **22** And when the days for their purification according to the law of Moses were completed, they brought Him up to Jerusalem to present Him to the Lord **23** (as it is written in the Law of the Lord, 'Every firstborn male that opens the womb shall be called holy to the Lord'), **24** and to offer a sacrifice according to what was said in the Law of the Lord, 'A pair of turtledoves or two young pigeons.'

25 And there was a man in Jerusalem whose name was Simeon; and this man was righteous and devout, looking for the consolation of Israel; and the Holy Spirit was upon him. **26** And it had been revealed to him by the Holy Spirit that he would not see death before he had seen the Lord's Christ. **27** And he came in the Spirit into the temple; and when the parents brought in the child Jesus, to carry out for Him the custom of the Law, **28** then he took Him into his arms, and blessed God, and said,

29 'Now Lord, You are releasing Your bond-servant to depart in peace, According to Your word;

30 For my eyes have seen Your salvation,

31 Which You have prepared in the presence of all peoples,

32 A Light of revelation to the Gentiles, And the glory of Your people Israel.'

33 And His father and mother were amazed at the things which were being said about Him. **34** And Simeon blessed them and said to Mary His mother, 'Behold, this Child is appointed for the fall and rise of many in Israel, and for a sign to be opposed— **35** and a sword will pierce even your own soul—to the end that thoughts from many hearts may be revealed.'

36 And there was a prophetess, Anna the daughter of Phanuel, of the tribe of Asher. She was advanced in years and had lived with her husband seven years after her marriage, **37** and then as a widow to the age of eighty-four. She never left the temple, serving night and day with fastings and prayers. **38** At that very moment she came up and began giving thanks to God, and continued to speak of Him to all those who were looking for the redemption of Jerusalem."

1. What can be inferred about the social status and spiritual devotion of Mary and Joseph from verses 21–24? (see Leviticus 12)

2. Who is Simeon (vv. 25–28)? What did he proclaim that is important to the Church today? (vv. 30–32) How does his declaration expand on what has already been revealed about the coming Son of God? (vv. 30–32, 34–35)

3. What is significant about his words to Mary in verse 34?

4. Where is the Holy Spirit in this passage? How is He at work?

5. Write down what is known about Anna (vv. 36–38). How did she respond to the arrival of Jesus?

NOTE: A prophet or prophetess was someone who was used by God to communicate His message to the world, and they would speak the words God put in their mouths. Often they would warn of judgment, call the people to repentance, and sometimes foretell the future pointing to the Messiah.

6. Why do you think these two encounters are recorded?

Application

How well do you wait on the Lord? Like Simeon, do you trust He is working when you see no evidence? Do you know anyone who "waits well?" Why do you think that is?

STUDY FIVE
The Childhood of Jesus

Based on the songs we sing at certain times of year, sometimes it seems the wise men's mark on history is who they were, how much they gave, and how far they travelled. Is our tendency to focus on their status and gifts a reflection of what matters most to us rather than what matters to God? Consider Mary and Joseph upon finding Jesus still in the temple after an emotional, three-day search. What mattered most to them was getting their son back. But Jesus had a different perspective. For Him, it was better to be in His Father's house than anywhere else. We relate to Jesus' frazzled earthly parents—much like us, when it is hard to see the end from the beginning, they "did not understand." Our heavenly Father delights in joyful hearts that rest in and worship Him. The wise ones in this story understood that. Do you?

Matthew 2:1–23

"Now after Jesus was born in Bethlehem of Judea in the days of Herod the king, magi from the east arrived in Jerusalem, saying, **2** 'Where is He who has been born King of the Jews? For we saw His star in the east and have come to worship Him.' **3** When Herod the king heard this, he was troubled, and all Jerusalem with him. **4** Gathering together all the chief priests and scribes of the people, he inquired of them where the Messiah was to be born. **5** They said to him, 'In Bethlehem of Judea; for this is what has been written by the prophet:

6 'And you, Bethlehem, land of Judah,
Are by no means least among the leaders of Judah;
For out of you shall come forth a Ruler
Who will shepherd My people Israel.'"

7 Then Herod secretly called the magi and determined from them the exact time the star appeared. **8** And he sent them to Bethlehem and said, 'Go and search carefully for the Child; and when you have found Him, report to me, so that I too may come and worship Him.' **9** After hearing the king, they went their way; and the star, which they had seen in the east, went on before them until it came and stood over the place where the Child was. **10** When they saw the star, they rejoiced exceedingly with great joy. **11** After coming into the house they saw the Child with Mary His mother; and they fell to the ground and worshiped Him. Then, opening their treasures, they presented to Him gifts of gold, frankincense, and myrrh. **12** And having been warned by God in a dream not to return to Herod, the magi left for their own country by another way.

13 Now when they had gone, behold, an angel of the Lord appeared to Joseph in a dream and said, 'Get up! Take the Child and His mother and flee to Egypt, and remain there until I tell you; for Herod is going to search for the Child to destroy Him.'

14 So Joseph got up and took the Child and His mother while it was still night, and left for Egypt. **15** He remained there until the death of Herod. This was to fulfill what had been spoken by the Lord through the prophet: 'Out of Egypt I called My Son.'

16 Then when Herod saw that he had been tricked by the magi, he became very enraged, and sent and slew all the male children who were in Bethlehem and all its vicinity, from two years old and under, according to the time which he had determined from the magi. **17** Then what had been spoken through Jeremiah the prophet was fulfilled:

18 "A voice was heard in Ramah,
Weeping and great mourning,
Rachel weeping for her children;
And she refused to be comforted,
Because they were no more."

19 But when Herod died, behold, an angel of the Lord appeared in a dream to Joseph in Egypt, and said, **20** 'Get up, take the Child and His mother, and go into the land of Israel; for those who sought the Child's life are dead.' **21** So Joseph got up, took the Child and His mother, and came into the land of Israel. **22** But when he heard that Archelaus was reigning over Judea in place of his father Herod, he was afraid to go there. Then after being warned by God in a dream, he left for the regions of Galilee, **23** and came and lived in a city called Nazareth. This was to fulfill what was spoken through the prophets: 'He shall be called a Nazarene.'"

1. What is believed about the Magi/wise men from tradition? What is known from this passage?

NOTE: Some scholars believe these men may have been astrologers from Babylonia whose ancestors had been greatly influenced by Daniel 400 years earlier. Daniel gave specific prophecies concerning the Messiah and was in a position of great authority during that time. For further investigation see the book of Daniel.

2. Why were the wise men (Gentiles) seeking Jesus (v. 2)? Why was King Herod (Jews) seeking Jesus (v. 13)?

3. How did the Magi/wise men respond to seeing the star? And to seeing Jesus? Why do you think they felt this way?

4. Where were Jesus and His family when the Magi found them?

NOTE: This indicates that some time had passed—perhaps up to about two years. They may have chosen to stay in Bethlehem because it was their ancestral city. It was also close to the temple, which the Jews believed was the dwelling place of God.

5. How did Herod respond to the news that he had been deceived by the Magi?

6. How did God protect His Son and family from King Herod and what role did Joseph play?

Imagine what it would have been like to be running from the Roman army in an effort to protect your child: an unarmed young couple with a baby, fleeing from the most well-trained army in the world at that time.

7. How do you see the sovereignty of God working in these circumstances?

Application

Do you remember a time when God protected you from harm? What did you learn?

A VISIT TO JERUSALEM

Luke 2:39–52

"³⁹ When they had performed everything according to the Law of the Lord, they returned to Galilee, to their own city of Nazareth. ⁴⁰ The Child continued to grow and become strong, increasing in wisdom; and the grace of God was upon Him.

⁴¹ Now His parents went to Jerusalem every year at the Feast of the Passover. ⁴² And when He became twelve, they went up there according to the custom of the Feast; ⁴³ and as they were returning, after spending the full number of days, the boy Jesus stayed behind in Jerusalem. But His parents were unaware of it, ⁴⁴ but supposed Him to be in the caravan, and went a day's journey; and they began looking for Him among their relatives and acquaintances. ⁴⁵ When they did not find Him, they returned to Jerusalem looking for Him. ⁴⁶ Then, after three days they found Him in the temple, sitting in the midst of the teachers, both listening to them and asking them questions. ⁴⁷ And all who heard Him were amazed at His understanding and His answers. ⁴⁸ When they saw Him, they were astonished; and His mother said to Him, 'Son, why have You treated us this way? Behold, Your father and I have been anxiously looking for You.' ⁴⁹ And He said to them, 'Why is it that you were looking for Me? Did you not know that I had to be in My Father's house?' ⁵⁰ But they did not understand the statement which He had made to them. ⁵¹ And He went down with them and came to Nazareth, and He continued in subjection to them; and His mother treasured all these things in her heart.

⁵² And Jesus kept increasing in wisdom and stature, and in favor with God and men."

1. How does this passage describe Jesus?

2. What does Scripture say about the Feast of the Passover? (What does it commemorate? How is it celebrated? Why is Israel commanded to celebrate it? Exodus 12–13)

3. Imagine Mary and Joseph as they discovered Jesus was missing and searched for Him. How long did it take Mary and Joseph to find Jesus? Where had He been and what was He doing when they found Him? What might their emotional state have been like?

4. Luke says Jesus' parents did not understand His response to Mary's questions. What did He say? What was the deeper meaning behind His answer to His earthly parents?

5. How does Hebrews 5:8 and Philippians 2:6–8 relate to Jesus' response to the earthly authority in His life? Does it have any connection to the description of Jesus in this passage? If so, what is it?

Application

Jesus didn't grow up in the limelight, as the longed-for Messiah and miracle worker. He grew up in obscurity, learning and growing. God's timing is perfect. Record a time when God's timing was not yours, yet proved to be perfect. What did you learn about God as a Promise Keeper?

A DEEPER LOOK

What happens when we seek Jesus?

Matthew 6:33   Colossians 3:1–4

WRAPPING UP

The people in the genealogy of Christ were less than perfect, but God chose them to be in the line of His Son's earthly family. The men and women of the Christmas story were flawed as well—overwhelmed and distracted, filled with fear and doubt. The angel announced to Joseph that Jesus was coming to save His people from their sins—a people who were imperfect. Into all our brokenness and failure, God sent His perfect Son.

Salvation through Jesus Christ provides a way for us to have an eternal relationship with our Creator. Christ didn't come to improve our lives; He came to be with us so that we could be with Him. He came to give us new hearts, from stone to flesh. Filled with power for love and grace and joy and peace. We are healed in the place of our deepest need. We are being renewed day by day. The old has gone; the new has come!

~ Map of John the Baptist ~

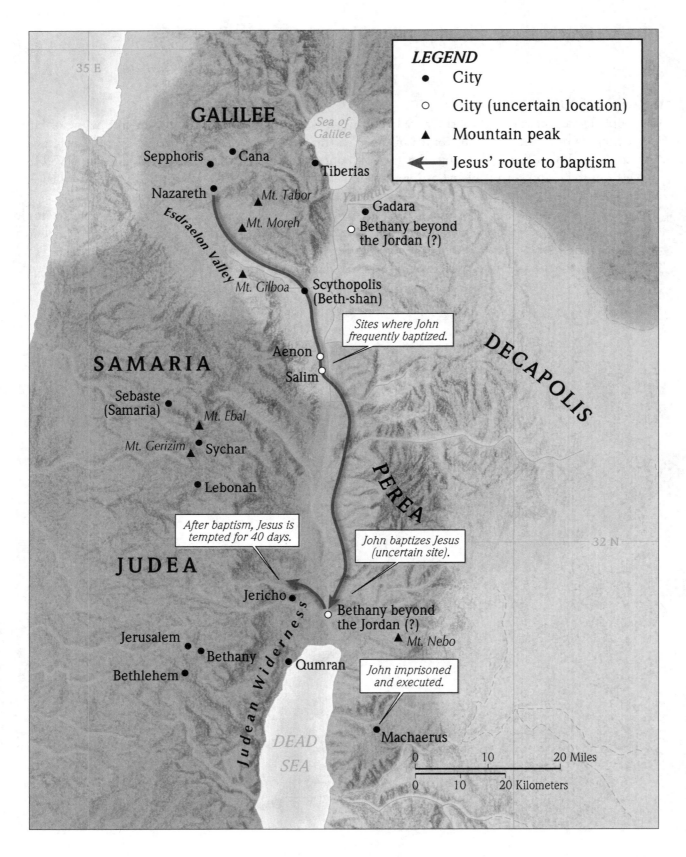

LEGEND
- City
- City (uncertain location)
- Mountain peak
- Jesus' route to baptism

GALILEE

Sea of Galilee

Sepphoris • Cana
Tiberias
Nazareth
Mt. Tabor
Gadara
Mt. Moreh
Bethany beyond the Jordan (?)

Esdraelon Valley

DECAPOLIS

Mt. Gilboa
Scythopolis (Beth-shan)

Sites where John frequently baptized.

SAMARIA

Aenon
Salim

Sebaste (Samaria)
Mt. Ebal
Mt. Gerizim • Sychar

PEREA

Lebonah

After baptism, Jesus is tempted for 40 days.

John baptizes Jesus (uncertain site).

JUDEA

Jericho
Bethany beyond the Jordan (?)
Mt. Nebo

Jerusalem • Bethany
Qumran

John imprisoned and executed.

Bethlehem

Judean Wilderness

DEAD SEA

Machaerus

| 0 | 10 | 20 Miles |
| 0 | 10 | 20 Kilometers |

JESUS, LAMB OF GOD

*"The next day he saw Jesus coming to him and said,
'Behold, the Lamb of God who takes away the sin of the world.'"*
JOHN 1:29

When John the Baptist publicly proclaimed Jesus to be the "Lamb of God," it would have been startling. To the Jewish ears hearing this title, a "lamb" evoked the rites and statutes required by the Mosaic law; particularly, the unblemished lamb that was sacrificed during each Passover (Exodus 12).

How is this man, they must have wondered, *part of the sacrifices God gave us through Moses? How can a man satisfy the Lord in the place of a lamb?*

The story in Genesis 22 might have helped it make sense to them. Their nation's father, Abraham, also pointed to Christ as the Lamb 4,000 years ago when, in obedience, he took his only son Isaac to be sacrificed as an offering to the LORD. "God will provide for himself the lamb…" he told Isaac (Genesis 22:8). Abraham spoke these words in faith for the moment, and is speaking just as clearly in this moment, as Jesus enters history.

Just as the Lord provided the ram in the thicket (Gen. 22:13), so He sent His Son to earth. Why? John declared the greater purpose of this Lamb in his next breath: *to take away the sins of the world.* The Jews slaughtered lambs every year in remembrance of their deliverance from the Angel of Death who "passed over" their blood-striped houses in Egypt (Exodus 12:12–13, 23). As the perfect Lamb, Jesus willingly offered Himself to die on the cross once for all, forever delivering us from the power of sin and death. And granting us a life of joy and peace with God here and now.

In His baptism, temptation, and miracles, Jesus walked in perfect obedience—a fragrant offering and sacrifice to God (Ephesians 5:2). Jesus demonstrated what it looks like to live in the flesh, dependent on the Spirit, in right relationship to the Father. Behold the Lamb of God this week and see Him as Redeemer, Deliverer, Provider, Promise, and Hope.

STUDY ONE
The Preaching of John the Baptist

"Scruffy looking" is the phrase that often comes to mind when we think of John the Baptist. And he probably was just that. But he was so much more! John was doing what no one else in his day bothered to do: fearlessly proclaiming God's truth and calling all Israel to public, heart-level repentance. And they responded en masse. The Jordan River was overflowing with sinners aware of their deep need, desperate for a life free from the burden of the law. John never strayed from his message—not only the call to confess and repent, but the greater promise that this was just the beginning.

Matthew 3:1-12
"Now in those days John the Baptist came, preaching in the wilderness of Judea, saying, **2** 'Repent, for the kingdom of heaven is at hand.' **3** For this is the one referred to by Isaiah the prophet when he said,

'The voice of one crying in the wilderness,
'Make ready the way of the Lord,
Make His paths straight!'
4 Now John himself had a garment of camel's hair and a leather belt around his waist; and his food was locusts and wild honey. **5** Then Jerusalem was going out to him, and all Judea and all the district around the Jordan; **6** and they were being baptized by him in the Jordan River, as they confessed their sins.
7 But when he saw many of the Pharisees and Sadducees coming for baptism, he said to them, 'You brood of vipers, who warned you to flee from the wrath to come? **8** Therefore bear fruit in keeping with repentance; **9** and do not suppose that you can say to yourselves, 'We have Abraham for our father'; for I say to you that from these stones God is able to raise up children to Abraham. **10** The axe is already laid at the root of the trees; therefore every tree that does not bear good fruit is cut down and thrown into the fire.
11 'As for me, I baptize you with water for repentance, but He who is coming after me is mightier than I, and I am not fit to remove His sandals; He will baptize you with the Holy Spirit and fire. **12** His winnowing fork is in His hand, and He will thoroughly clear His threshing floor; and He will gather His wheat into the barn, but He will burn up the chaff with unquenchable fire.'"

1. Write down the description of John from Scripture. Where did his ministry take place? Why would that location have been significant for the Jews (Numbers 32:13)? What do these things tell us about John?

NOTE: There is no biblical record of other teachers baptizing for repentance of sins at this time in history. Notice that verses 5–6 describe John's following and influence as being widespread and in an almost revival-like context. See also Luke 3:10–14 for descriptions of the kinds of people who were drawn to John's ministry.

2. What was John's message? What did Isaiah in Matthew 3:3 foretell John's message would be? How are they similar?

3. John's baptism was a public event. Why was the act of baptism important in John's ministry?

4. Who is recorded as responding to John's teaching (v. 5)? What was the requirement of John's baptism (v. 6)?

5. Use an online Bible dictionary (try www.biblestudytools.com) and define Pharisees and Sadducees (often referred to in the Gospels as "the religious leaders") and write the definitions below. What does verse 7 tell us about why they came to John in the wilderness?

6. How does John describe the Pharisees and Sadducees? What warnings does he give them? What challenge did he give them in verse 8 (Lamentations 3:40 and Acts 26:20)? What does John say these religious leaders believe is their "ticket to heaven"? (v. 9)

7. How did John describe the difference between his ministry and the ministry of Jesus (vv. 11–12)?

Application

What is repentance? How is repentance different from guilt or regret? What difference does it make? Is repentance and confession a part of your walk with Jesus?

A DEEPER LOOK

Read the verses below and note what the Bible says about repentance. Write down truths that speak to you.

2 Chronicles 7:14   Psalms 51

Isaiah 30:15   2 Corinthians 7:9–10

Acts 3:19   James 4:8–10

Romans 2:3–5   1 John 1:8–10

 ## STUDY TWO
The Baptism of Jesus

If stage direction were inserted in Scripture, this passage would begin with, "Enter Jesus." His presence creates a tectonic shift in world events and in individual lives, starting with John the Baptist. Jesus, the Son of God, comes to His cousin on His own accord—not to relieve him of his duties or pat him on the back for his good work, but to submit Himself to be baptized by him. Jesus stood in the same waters as the men and women who actually had sins to confess and took His first steps toward the cross. In this moment, Jesus "was numbered with the transgressors." (Isaiah 53:12)

Matthew 3:13–17
"**13** Then Jesus arrived from Galilee at the Jordan coming to John, to be baptized by him. **14** But John tried to prevent Him, saying, 'I have need to be baptized by You, and do You come to me?' **15** But Jesus answering said to him, 'Permit it at this time; for in this way it is fitting for us to fulfill all righteousness.' Then he permitted Him. **16** After being baptized, Jesus came up immediately from the water; and behold, the heavens were opened, and he saw the Spirit of God descending as a dove and lighting on Him, **17** and behold, a voice out of the heavens said, 'This is My beloved Son, in whom I am well-pleased.'"

1. In your own words, write down what happened in verses 13–15.

2. Matthew 3:6 says the people were confessing their sins as they were being baptized. This could not have been true for Jesus, the perfect Son of God, nor was repentance His reason for baptism. Why did Jesus present Himself for baptism (v. 15; see also 2 Corinthians 5:21, Romans 8:3)?

3. Describe what happened immediately after Jesus' baptism in verses 16–17. (See also Isaiah 42:1)

4. What sort of images does the picture of a dove bring to mind?

5. Where is the Trinity (Father, Son, and Holy Spirit) in this passage? Can you think of any other times in Scripture where the Trinity is "visibly/audibly" present all together?

6. How does God the Father respond to His Son's baptism? Why is this important?

Application

Have you ever been baptized? Write down your understanding of what baptism symbolizes. Why is it important for believers in Christ to be baptized?

STUDY THREE
The Temptation of Jesus

The Lamb of God is led into the wilderness to experience what is common to all of us—the unrelenting assault of our oldest adversary, Satan. It is easy to forget how well the devil knows the heart and mind of man. He is patient and crafty and more foul and depraved than all the evil ever witnessed on earth. And somehow—for our sake—Jesus allows him to stand in His presence. Imagine yourself at your most vulnerable—hungry, lonely, tired, and antagonized by temptation. Jesus felt all of that and had the right and power to call down the hosts of heaven. Yet He endured. This is what the writer of Hebrews means when he reminds us, *"For we do not have a high priest who cannot sympathize with our weaknesses, but One who has been tempted in all things as we are, yet without sin. Therefore let us draw near with confidence to the throne of grace, so that we may receive mercy and find grace to help in time of need."* (Hebrews 4:15–16)

Matthew 4:1–11
"Then Jesus was led up by the Spirit into the wilderness to be tempted by the devil. **2** And after He had fasted forty days and forty nights, He then became hungry. **3** And the tempter came and said to Him, 'If You are the Son of God, command that these stones become bread.' **4** But He answered and said, 'It is written, 'Man shall not live on bread alone, but on every word that proceeds out of the mouth of God.'

5 Then the devil took Him into the holy city and had Him stand on the pinnacle of the temple, **6** and said to Him, 'If You are the Son of God, throw Yourself down; for it is written,

'He will command His angels concerning You';
and
'On their hands they will bear You up,
So that You will not strike Your foot against a stone.'

7 Jesus said to him, 'On the other hand, it is written, 'You shall not put the Lord your God to the test.'

8 Again, the devil took Him to a very high mountain and showed Him all the kingdoms of the world and their glory; **9** and he said to Him, 'All these things I will give You, if You fall down and worship me.' **10** Then Jesus said to him, 'Go, Satan! For it is written, 'You shall worship the Lord your God, and serve Him only.' **11** Then the devil left Him; and behold, angels came and began to minister to Him."

1. Why did Jesus have to endure temptation? (Hebrews 4:15) What was the purpose of Jesus' temptation? (Philippians 2:6–8)

2. Where and when did the temptation happen? Who led Jesus there? Describe what the landscape could have looked like.

3. How long had Jesus been fasting? Remembering that Jesus was fully human, what kind of physical shape would He be in after this length of time?

4. List the things Satan tempted Jesus with. Why do you think he tempted Jesus in those specific ways?

5. What is the difference between Satan's and Jesus' knowledge of Scripture?

6. What does Scripture say about the domain of Satan? (Job 1:6–7, 2:1–2)

7. How is the scene of Christ's temptation a model for believers?

8. Read Psalms 91:11, the passage Satan referred to in his conversation with Jesus. How is this actually fulfilled in this scene in the wilderness?

9. How does this scene prove Jesus as an acceptable Lamb?

Application
What does Satan specifically tempt you with? What does that say about how well he knows you and how dangerous he is? (1 Peter 5:8–9)

A DEEPER LOOK
1 John 2:16 says, "For all that is in the world, the lust of the flesh and the lust of the eyes and the boastful pride of life, is not from the Father, but is from the world."

Describe how Jesus' temptations in the wilderness fall into these three categories. How might have these false promises been tempting to Jesus both immediately and with the future in mind?

Do you ever find yourself longing to trade your life (or your spouse or your bank account) with someone else? What possession of your neighbor's are you envious of? When and where in your life do you feel superior to others?

How does 1 John 2:16 give us hope in the midst of temptation?

STUDY FOUR
The Testimony of John the Baptist

John was being used in a mighty way in the nation of Israel before Christ appeared. The fact that a delegation was sent to discuss his status indicates John had the attention of much of the Jewish world at the time. He was famous, but he always knew his place. He knew his ministry, while important and ordained, was temporary, pointing to something complete and permanent. When asked, "Who are you?," John could have taken advantage of the self-promoting opportunity. Instead, he humbly says, "Don't look at me—there's nothing to see. I'm just a voice. See the One who has chosen to stand in our midst, entering humanity from eternity. I'm not even good enough to take the shoes off His feet!" John prepared his disciples for life beyond his ministry, and many willingly—joyfully—followed the One who promised even greater things.

John 1:19-51
"**19** This is the testimony of John, when the Jews sent to him priests and Levites from Jerusalem to ask him, 'Who are you?' **20** And he confessed and did not deny, but confessed, 'I am not the Christ.' **21** They asked him, 'What then? Are you Elijah?' And he said, 'I am not.' 'Are you the Prophet?' And he answered, 'No.' **22** Then they said to him, 'Who are you, so that we may give an answer to those who sent us? What do you say about yourself?' **23** He said, 'I am a voice of one crying in the wilderness, "Make straight the way of the Lord," as Isaiah the prophet said.'

24 Now they had been sent from the Pharisees. **25** They asked him, and said to him, 'Why then are you baptizing, if you are not the Christ, nor Elijah, nor the Prophet?' **26** John answered them saying, 'I baptize in water, but among you stands One whom you do not know. **27** It is He who comes after me, the thong of whose sandal I am not worthy to untie.' **28** These things took place in Bethany beyond the Jordan, where John was baptizing. **29** The next day he saw Jesus coming to him and said, 'Behold, the Lamb of God who takes away the sin of the world! **30** This is He on behalf of whom I said, 'After me comes a Man who has a higher rank than I, for He existed before me.' **31** I did not recognize Him, but so that He might be manifested to Israel, I came baptizing in water.' **32** John testified saying, 'I have seen the Spirit descending as a dove out of heaven, and He remained upon Him. **33** I did not recognize Him, but He who sent me to baptize in water said to me, 'He upon whom you see the Spirit descending and remaining upon Him, this is the One who baptizes in the Holy Spirit.' **34** I myself have seen, and have testified that this is the Son of God."

35 Again the next day John was standing with two of his disciples, **36** and he looked at Jesus as He walked, and said, 'Behold, the Lamb of God!' **37** The two disciples heard him speak, and they followed Jesus. **38** And Jesus turned and saw them following, and said to them, 'What do you seek?' They said to Him, 'Rabbi (which translated means Teacher), where are You staying?' **39** He said to them, 'Come, and you will see.' So they came and saw where He was staying; and they stayed with Him that day, for it was about the tenth hour. **40** One of the two who heard John speak and followed Him, was Andrew, Simon Peter's brother. **41** He found first his own brother Simon and said to him, 'We have found the Messiah' (which translated means Christ). **42** He brought him to Jesus. Jesus looked at him and said, 'You are Simon the son of John; you shall be called Cephas' (which is translated Peter).

43 The next day He purposed to go into Galilee, and He found Philip. And Jesus said to him, 'Follow Me.' **44** Now Philip was from Bethsaida, of the city of Andrew and Peter. **45** Philip found Nathanael and said to him, 'We have found Him of whom Moses in the Law and also the Prophets wrote—Jesus of Nazareth, the son of Joseph.' **46** Nathanael said to him, 'Can any good thing come out of Nazareth?' Philip said to him, "Come and see." **47** Jesus saw Nathanael coming to Him, and said of him, 'Behold, an Israelite indeed, in whom there is no deceit!' **48** Nathanael said to Him, 'How do You know me?' Jesus answered and said to him, 'Before Philip called you, when you were under the fig tree, I saw you.' **49** Nathanael answered Him, 'Rabbi, You are the Son of God; You are the King of Israel.' **50** Jesus answered and said to him, 'Because I said to you that I saw you under the fig tree, do you believe? You will see greater things than these.' **51** And He said to him, 'Truly, truly, I say to you, you will see the heavens opened and the angels of God ascending and descending on the Son of Man.'"

1. To whom does this passage say John gave testimony about Jesus? What did the delegation ask John in verse 19?

2. What was the delegation's specific accusation against John in verse 25?

3. Who does John say he is? Who does John say he is not?

4. How does John acknowledge the preexistence of Christ in this scene? (v. 30)

5. What does verse 31 say about John's knowledge of Jesus prior to His baptism? What further explanation of Jesus' baptism does John give in this verse?

6. What is the difference between how John testified about Jesus in verses 19–28 and in verses 29–34? What crucial revelation took place in verse 33? How does John fulfill his ministry in verse 34?

7. What did John say the Spirit of God did in verses 32 and 33 (Isaiah 11:2, 61:1)?

8. How is John fulfilling his ministry in verses 35–37? What do we learn in verse 41 is the reason these men made their decision?

9. Compare and contrast the "recruitment" of disciples in verses 35–42 and verses 43–51. What additional revelation about Jesus did Philip provide (v. 45)?

10. What was Nathanael's initial response to Jesus in verse 46? How did Jesus receive Nathanael in verse 47? What role did Philip play (vv. 45–46)?

11. As His ministry begins and His following grows, various names and descriptions for Jesus are recorded by John in this section of scripture. Read back through verses 19–51 and circle all the words and phrases referring to Jesus. What could John's purpose have been in using so many descriptions for Jesus?

Application

In this passage, John is very clear about who he is and who Jesus is. The Pharisees' religion was a stumbling block for them. How does "religion" keep people from seeing Jesus and the grace He freely offers?

A DEEPER LOOK

The verses below are about sacrifice: Christ's for us and, also, sacrifices that are pleasing to Him. Read through them and then choose one to meditate on and memorize. Record any observations. Consider and pray through the interpretation—to the readers then and now. And pray for the Holy Spirit to give you specific applications for your life.

Hosea 6:6   Romans 5:8

Psalms 51:16–17   Romans 12:1

John 3:16   Hebrews 9:26–28

Acts 20:24   Hebrews 13:15–16

Romans 3:25   Ephesians 5:1–2

STUDY FIVE
The First Miracle of Jesus

Why Mary came to Jesus to solve this problem is unclear. Perhaps it was simply faith, grown from the seeds of all she had treasured in her heart up until now. To human ears, Jesus' words to His mother might sound harsh. Imagine them, instead, as a firm yet tender reproof. Rather than impatience or exasperation, hear the gentleness of a lamb in His voice. Remember, this is no ordinary Son, and so His response would most likely have been extraordinary. Extraordinarily kind and gracious to His earthly mother who wanted so much to understand and yet, like us, her own agenda and expectations caused her to forget Who she was talking to. What a strange experience, this role reversal. Mary stands before the Second Person of the Trinity, talking to Him as her Child and in return, He responds as a loving Father.

John 2:1–12

"On the third day there was a wedding in Cana of Galilee, and the mother of Jesus was there; **2** and both Jesus and His disciples were invited to the wedding. **3** When the wine ran out, the mother of Jesus said to Him, 'They have no wine.' **4** And Jesus said to her, 'Woman, what does that have to do with us? My hour has not yet come.' **5** His mother said to the servants, 'Whatever He says to you, do it.' **6** Now there were six stone waterpots set there for the Jewish custom of purification, containing twenty or thirty gallons each. **7** Jesus said to them, 'Fill the waterpots with water.' So they filled them up to the brim. **8** And He said to them, 'Draw some out now and take it to the headwaiter.' So they took it to him. **9** When the headwaiter tasted the water which had become wine, and did not know where it came from (but the servants who had drawn the water knew), the headwaiter called the bridegroom, **10** and said to him, 'Every man serves the good wine first, and when the people have drunk freely, then he serves the poorer wine; but you have kept the good wine until now.' **11** This beginning of His signs Jesus did in Cana of Galilee, and manifested His glory, and His disciples believed in Him.

12 After this He went down to Capernaum, He and His mother and His brothers and His disciples; and they stayed there a few days."

1. According to the passage, who attended the wedding at Cana? What does Jesus' invitation to and presence at a wedding say about Him?

2. What does the phrase, "My hour has not yet come" refer to? (see John 7:30; 8:20; 12:23, 27; 13:1; 17:1)

3. How does Jesus meet a need in this story? How does Jesus bring glory to Himself in this story?

4. What attributes of God are evident in this scene?

5. Read these passages and note how wine is connected to joy in Scripture: Isaiah 25:6–8; Jeremiah 31:12–13; Amos 9:13–15.

 NOTE: Notice in each passage the celebration and joy of people who return to the Lord.

6. What is the purpose for the miracles Jesus did in His life on earth? (v. 11)

Application

Who do you turn to first when you have a problem? Is there anything you need to do differently when a trial or crisis comes? What are some things you can do to help you fix your eyes on Jesus?

WRAPPING UP

We started this week beholding the Lamb of God through the eyes of His cousin, John, then watched Jesus obediently endure testing and trials as His ministry began. The truth of Jesus as God's perfect Lamb is rooted in the Old Testament, beginning with Abraham and Isaac and appearing again with the Israelites in the wilderness. Spotless lambs were an integral part of the rites of remembrance and worship in Israel, culminating each year in the celebration of Passover. So, from the beginning of God's people, the lamb has always been connected to sacrifice.

The Lamb of God—Jesus—made the ultimate sacrifice for us: He willingly took on our sin and God's wrath through His death on the cross. And unlike the millions of lambs slaughtered for sacrifices through the ages, this perfect Lamb died once for all. And He conquered death and lives today! Jesus has made the way for us to draw near to God, now and in eternity (Hebrews 7:23–28; Hebrews 10:11–14). Praise His holy name!

~ Map of the Samaritan Well ~

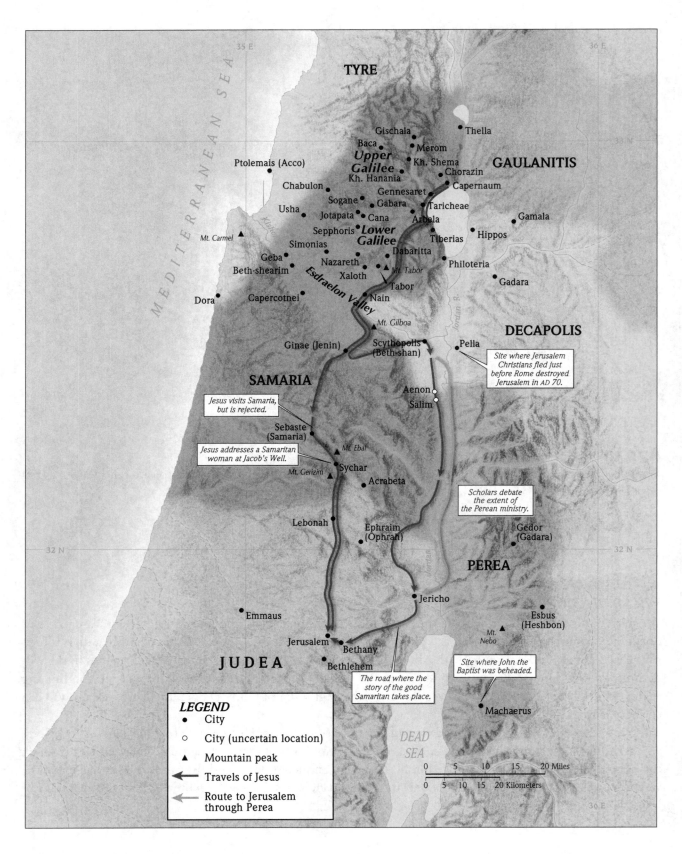

MEDITERRANEAN SEA

TYRE

Gischala
Thella
Baca
Merom
Upper Galilee
Kh. Shema
GAULANITIS
Ptolemais (Acco)
Kh. Hanania
Chorazin
Capernaum
Chabulon
Gennesaret
Sogane
Gabara
Taricheae
Gamala
Usha
Jotapata
Cana
Arbela
Simonias
Sepphoris
Lower Galilee
Tiberias
Hippos
Mt. Carmel
Dabaritta
Geba
Nazareth
Xaloth
Mt. Tabor
Philoteria
Beth-shearim
Esdraelon Valley
Tabor
Gadara
Dora
Capercotnei
Nain
Mt. Gilboa
DECAPOLIS
Ginae (Jenin)
Scythopolis (Beth-shan)
Pella

Site where Jerusalem Christians fled just before Rome destroyed Jerusalem in AD 70.

SAMARIA
Aenon
Salim

Jesus visits Samaria, but is rejected.

Sebaste (Samaria)
Mt. Ebal

Jesus addresses a Samaritan woman at Jacob's Well.

Mt. Gerizim
Sychar
Acrabeta

Scholars debate the extent of the Perean ministry.

Lebonah
Ephraim (Ophrah)
Gedor (Gadara)

PEREA

Jericho
Esbus (Heshbon)
Emmaus
Mt. Nebo

Jerusalem
Bethany

JUDEA
Bethlehem

Site where John the Baptist was beheaded.

The road where the story of the good Samaritan takes place.

Machaerus

DEAD SEA

LEGEND
- City
- City (uncertain location)
- Mountain peak
- Travels of Jesus
- Route to Jerusalem through Perea

0   5   10   15   20 Miles
0 5 10 15 20 Kilometers

JESUS, THE MESSIAH

"The woman said to Him, 'I know that Messiah is coming
(He who is called Christ); when that One comes, He will declare
all things to us.' Jesus said to her, 'I who speak to you am He.'"
JOHN 4:25–26

t is easy to think that, had we lived in the time of Jesus, we would have seen His miracles, heard His teaching, remembered the prophecies, and believed Jesus was the long-awaited Messiah. But Scripture seems to tell a different story. His own disciples, family, and closest friends doubted He was who He claimed to be. The religious leaders — men who spent their lives studying the law and prophets — never recognized Who was standing right before their eyes. It was, as will be seen this week, the least likely "converts" that had the greatest faith.

Messiah means "Anointed One." Anointing was reserved for the offices of prophet, priest, and king among God's people. Jesus fulfills all these roles perfectly and permanently.

As Prophet, Jesus reveals and communicates God's truth to God's people (Matthew 11:27; Matthew 13:57; John 12:49). As Priest, Jesus gave Himself as a once-for-all sacrifice to purify His people from sin (Ephesians 5:2; Hebrews 10:11–14). As King, Jesus has all authority to rule and reign over the creation that He brought into existence (Zechariah 9:9; Matthew 27:11; Colossians 2:16–17). He is the only One who can complete and accomplish all of this as our one true Savior and Lord.

If any questions remain for you about who Jesus is, consider His claims to be the Messiah this week. He is the Light who entered the darkness. He is from above and above all from eternity past. He is the Living Water Who gives eternal life. He is the fulfillment of Scripture and the only begotten Son of God. He is the long-awaited Messiah.

STUDY ONE
First Passover — Cleansing of the Temple

This scene in Scripture can be unsettling. Turning over tables and wielding a handmade whip is not the picture of Jesus tacked to our Sunday school walls. This is Jesus' first trip to the temple recorded in John's Gospel, and He's not there to teach or heal or perform miracles. The Messiah is consumed with zeal — an intense passion or fiery devotion — over what He sees: the misuse and abuse of His Father's house, the temple. The word "cleansing" is not seen in the passage itself, but it is what Jesus was doing — removing the stain of greed left by the merchants and money changers, and restoring glory to the dwelling place of God's presence.

John 2:13–25

"13 The Passover of the Jews was near, and Jesus went up to Jerusalem. 14 And He found in the temple those who were selling oxen and sheep and doves, and the money changers seated at their tables. 15 And He made a scourge of cords, and drove them all out of the temple, with the sheep and the oxen; and He poured out the coins of the money changers and overturned their tables; 16 and to those who were selling the doves He said, 'Take these things away; stop making My Father's house a place of business.' 17 His disciples remembered that it was written, 'Zeal for Your house will consume me.' 18 The Jews then said to Him, 'What sign do You show us as your authority for doing these things?' 19 Jesus answered them, 'Destroy this temple, and in three days I will raise it up.' 20 The Jews then said, 'It took forty-six years to build this temple, and will You raise it up in three days?' 21 But He was speaking of the temple of His body. 22 So when He was raised from the dead, His disciples remembered that He said this; and they believed the Scripture and the word which Jesus had spoken.

23 Now when He was in Jerusalem at the Passover, during the feast, many believed in His name, observing His signs which He was doing. 24 But Jesus, on His part, was not entrusting Himself to them, for He knew all men, 25 and because He did not need anyone to testify concerning man, for He Himself knew what was in man."

1. What time of year does Jesus make His way to Jerusalem? Who does He find at the temple? Considering the time and place, who should He first encounter there?

NOTE: Scholars say this marketplace was set up in the Court of the Gentiles, an area located in the outer court of the temple compound reserved for non-Jews to worship and pray. The merchants overcharged for their "certified" animals, extorting those who came to worship the Lord. And the temple priests lined their pockets with the fees they required for the privilege of selling there.

2. What were they doing?

3. What four things did Jesus do? What did He say?

4. How did the disciples respond to Jesus? How did the Jews respond?

5. What attributes of God do you see on display in this passage?

6. Define *zeal*. How can it be misdirected (Romans 10:2, Galatians 1:13–14, Philippians 3:6)? How is it perfectly displayed in this scene?

7. What do verses 24–25 say about Jesus' omniscience and divine insight?

Application

Previous passages have called Jesus the "Lamb of God." In this scene, Jesus shows another aspect of His divine nature. What does this passage say to you about God's view of sin? What does it say to you about your own anger and response to offenses?

 **STUDY TWO**
You Must Be Born Again

As a Pharisee, it was unusual for Nicodemus to seek a private audience with Jesus. "Pharisee" means "separatist;" in self-righteousness, Pharisees set themselves apart from and above the world around them. Called a "brood of vipers" by John (Matthew 3:7), they were counting on their religious adherence to laws—not a Messiah—to gain access to heaven. In every other interaction, this group of influential Jewish leaders expressed prideful opposition to Jesus as Messiah, and Jesus rebuked and condemned them. But this exchange reminds us that only Jesus knows the heart. As the Son of God patiently engaged Nicodemus, He introduced the idea of being "born again"—a term never used before—and even presented the Gospel to Nicodemus, that he might believe: *"For God so loved the world that He gave His only Son. . . ."*

John 3:1-21

"Now there was a man of the Pharisees, named Nicodemus, a ruler of the Jews; **2** this man came to Jesus by night and said to Him, 'Rabbi, we know that You have come from God as a teacher; for no one can do these signs that You do unless God is with him.' **3** Jesus answered and said to him, 'Truly, truly, I say to you, unless one is born again he cannot see the kingdom of God.'

4 Nicodemus said to Him, 'How can a man be born when he is old? He cannot enter a second time into his mother's womb and be born, can he?' **5** Jesus answered, 'Truly, truly, I say to you, unless one is born of water and the Spirit he cannot enter into the kingdom of God. **6** That which is born of the flesh is flesh, and that which is born of the Spirit is spirit. **7** Do not be amazed that I said to you, 'You must be born again.' **8** The wind blows where it wishes and you hear the sound of it, but do not know where it comes from and where it is going; so is everyone who is born of the Spirit.'

9 Nicodemus said to Him, 'How can these things be?' **10** Jesus answered and said to him, 'Are you the teacher of Israel and do not understand these things? **11** Truly, truly, I say to you, we speak of what we know and testify of what we have seen, and you do not accept our testimony. **12** If I told you earthly things and you do not believe, how will you believe if I tell you heavenly things? **13** No one has ascended into heaven, but He who descended from heaven: the Son of Man. **14** As Moses lifted up the serpent in the wilderness, even so must the Son of Man be lifted up; **15** so that whoever believes will in Him have eternal life.

16 'For God so loved the world, that He gave His only begotten Son, that whoever believes in Him shall not perish, but have eternal life. **17** For God did not send the Son into the world to judge the world, but that the world might be saved through Him. **18** He who believes in Him is not judged; he who does not believe has been judged already, because he has not believed in the name of the only begotten Son of God. **19** This is the judgment, that the Light has come into the world, and men loved the darkness rather than the Light, for their deeds were evil. **20** For everyone who does evil hates the Light, and does not come to the Light for fear that his deeds will be exposed. **21** But he who practices the truth comes to the Light, so that his deeds may be manifested as having been wrought in God.'"

1. Write down what is revealed about Nicodemus—expressed or implied—in this passage.

2. What time of day did Nicodemus approach Jesus? What is significant about that?

NOTE: Chronologically, this meeting took place right after Jesus cleansed the temple.

3. How did Nicodemus describe Jesus? What questions did Nicodemus ask Jesus?

4. Charles Spurgeon said, "*Discernment is not knowing the difference between right and wrong. It is knowing the difference between right and almost right.*" How is this demonstrated in Nicodemus' assessment of who Jesus is in verse 2?

5. Write down repeated words, phrases, or ideas in Jesus' response to Nicodemus in verses 3–21. If repetition signals importance, what is Jesus emphasizing to Nicodemus? And to us?

6. How does Jesus explain His authority to speak as He has in verse 13?

7. What is Jesus foretelling in verses 14–15?

8. What did Nicodemus need? What is the greatest need of humanity? (vv. 16–18)

9. Does reading John 3:16 in the context of this encounter and conversation affect your view of this familiar verse? If so, how?

10. How does Jesus indict mankind in verse 19? What is the difference in the two types of people Jesus talks about in verses 20–21?

Application

Jesus' mission statement on earth is expressed in John 3:16–17. What is your mission in life? Does it line up with God's mission for you?

STUDY THREE
John's Last Testimony

As the disciples of John faithfully carried out the mission of baptism in Israel, their message spread and ministry grew. And now, they were partnered with Jesus Himself! But a self-serving attitude seeped in when a doctrinal argument caught their hearts off guard. And in the midst of vibrant ministry, conflict arose. The sins of self-righteousness and pride were kindling, waiting for just the right spark to set their jealousy ablaze. Here, John once against proves his leadership, drowning their distraction with a humble reminder: *He must increase, but I must decrease.* John calls himself "a friend of the bridegroom" — standing to the side, pointing to center stage, where the Messiah stands. John's lamp is fading as the Messiah's light grows. And that, John said, makes his joy complete.

John 3:22–26

"²² After these things Jesus and His disciples came into the land of Judea, and there He was spending time with them and baptizing. ²³ John also was baptizing in Aenon near Salim, because there was much water there; and people were coming and were being baptized— ²⁴ for John had not yet been thrown into prison.

²⁵ Therefore there arose a discussion on the part of John's disciples with a Jew about purification. ²⁶ And they came to John and said to him, 'Rabbi, He who was with you beyond the Jordan, to whom you have testified, behold, He is baptizing and all are coming to Him.' ²⁷ John answered and said, 'A man can receive nothing unless it has been given him from heaven. ²⁸ You yourselves are my witnesses that I said, 'I am not the Christ,' but, 'I have been sent ahead of Him.' ²⁹ He who has the bride is the bridegroom; but the friend of the bridegroom, who stands and hears him, rejoices greatly because of the bridegroom's voice. So this joy of mine has been made full. ³⁰ He must increase, but I must decrease.

³¹ 'He who comes from above is above all, he who is of the earth is from the earth and speaks of the earth. He who comes from heaven is above all. ³² What He has seen and heard, of that He testifies; and no one receives His testimony. ³³ He who has received His testimony has set his seal to this, that God is true. ³⁴ For He whom God has sent speaks the words of God; for He gives the Spirit without measure. ³⁵ The Father loves the Son and has given all things into His hand. ³⁶ He who believes in the Son has eternal life; but he who does not obey the Son will not see life, but the wrath of God abides on him.'"

1. What are "these things" (v. 22)?

2. Who was baptizing and where was it taking place? (see also John 4:2)

3. What is foreshadowed in verse 24?

4. What is happening in verses 25–26? How might Proverbs 16:27–28 apply to this scene?

5. How does John respond? What evidence of humility do you see on display in John's life in verses 27–30?

6. How was John's joy "been made full?"

7. List the comparisons and contrasts in this passage.

8. Write down any language in this passage that demonstrates the preexistence of Jesus.

9. Verse 30 is known as the summary statement of John's ministry. What was he saying?

Application

Where in your life do you need to say to yourself, "I am not the Christ" (v. 28)?

STUDY FOUR
Jesus and the Woman at the Well

The Messiah restored in different ways in this passage. To the woman at the well and the spurned Samaritan villagers, He restored hope. To the official's son in Cana, He restored life. The woman drawing water in the heat of the day was a social and spiritual outcast. The dying child was sick beyond what any treatment of man could touch. It was clear they all had needs greater than could be met by human strength and resources. Though we only see the results of one (v. 39), undoubtedly both testimonies impacted the lives of those around them. Jesus refreshes all who ask with the Living Water only He can give, drawn from the depths of His love, satisfying the needs of lives and hearts forever.

John 4:1–26

"Therefore when the Lord knew that the Pharisees had heard that Jesus was making and baptizing more disciples than John **2** (although Jesus Himself was not baptizing, but His disciples were), **3** He left Judea and went away again into Galilee. **4** And He had to pass through Samaria. **5** So He came to a city of Samaria called Sychar, near the parcel of ground that Jacob gave to his son Joseph; **6** and Jacob's well was there. So Jesus, being wearied from His journey, was sitting thus by the well. It was about the sixth hour.

7 There came a woman of Samaria to draw water. Jesus said to her, 'Give Me a drink.' **8** For His disciples had gone away into the city to buy food. **9** Therefore the Samaritan woman said to Him, 'How is it that You, being a Jew, ask me for a drink since I am a Samaritan woman?' (For Jews have no dealings with Samaritans.) **10** Jesus answered and said to her, 'If you knew the gift of God, and who it is who says to you, 'Give Me a drink,' you would have asked Him, and He would have given you living water.' **11** She said to Him, 'Sir, You have nothing to draw with and the well is deep; where then do You get that living water? **12** You are not greater than our father Jacob, are You, who gave us the well, and drank of it himself and his sons and his cattle?' **13** Jesus answered and said to her, 'Everyone who drinks of this water will thirst again; **14** but whoever drinks of the water that I will give him shall never thirst; but the water that I will give him will become in him a well of water springing up to eternal life.'

15 The woman said to Him, 'Sir, give me this water, so I will not be thirsty nor come all the way here to draw.' **16** He said to her, 'Go, call your husband and come here.' **17** The woman answered and said, 'I have no husband.' Jesus said to her, 'You have correctly said, 'I have no husband'; **18** for you have had five husbands, and the one whom you now have is not your husband; this you have said truly.' **19** The woman said to Him, 'Sir, I perceive that You are a prophet. **20** Our fathers worshiped in this mountain, and you people say that in Jerusalem is the place where men ought to worship.' **21** Jesus said to her, 'Woman, believe Me, an hour is coming when neither in this mountain nor in Jerusalem will you worship the Father. **22** You worship what you do not know; we worship what we know, for salvation is from the Jews. **23** But an hour is coming, and now is, when the true worshipers will worship the Father in spirit and truth; for such people the Father seeks to be His worshipers. **24** God is spirit, and those who worship Him must worship in spirit and truth.' **25** The woman said to Him, 'I know that Messiah is coming (He who is called Christ); when that One comes, He will declare all things to us.' **26** Jesus said to her, 'I who speak to you am He.'"

1. Describe what's happening in verses 1–3. Why do you think Jesus left Judea?

2. What is known about Samaria and Israel's relationship with it? Read 2 Kings 17, specifically verses 24–31, for some history.

3. Describe the humanity of Jesus seen in these verses.

4. Describe the deity of Jesus on display in these verses.

5. What is significant about the time of day in this passage?

NOTE: Scholars explain that the sixth hour is 6 p.m. by Roman time and 12 noon by Jewish time. In this context, the latter is likely.

6. Think back to Jesus' conversation with Nicodemus and to His conversation with the woman at the well.

   How are they similar?

How are they different?

How does each encounter resolve?

7. What are repeated words and phrases in this conversation? What are they pointing to?

8. What is the Samaritan woman most concerned with in verse 15 and why? Like Nicodemus, what is her greatest need?

9. What questions does the woman ask Jesus?

10. What do verses 16–18, 19–20, and 25 tell us about the woman?

11. What does Jesus clearly reveal to the woman in verse 26? Did Jesus do this for Nicodemus (John 3:12)?

Application

Like the Jews and Samaritans, do you find it difficult to love people who are different from you? How can Christ's love and acceptance of you motivate you to love when it is difficult?

A DEEPER LOOK

Have you ever been confronted with your sin? How did you respond?

Have you ever had to confront others with their sin? How well do you speak the truth in love to another believer?

For a biblical perspective on this dynamic, read the following passages. How do these verses instruct you in your relationships?

Ezra 9:1–15   2 Thessalonians 3:14–15

Psalms 141:5   2 Timothy 2:24–26

Proverbs 12:1   Hebrews 3:12–13

Matthew 18:15–17   James 5:19–20

Galatians 6:1

John 4:27–54

"**27** At this point His disciples came, and they were amazed that He had been speaking with a woman, yet no one said, 'What do You seek?' or, 'Why do You speak with her?' **28** So the woman left her waterpot, and went into the city and said to the men, **29** 'Come, see a man who told me all the things that I have done; this is not the Christ, is it?' **30** They went out of the city, and were coming to Him.

31 Meanwhile the disciples were urging Him, saying, 'Rabbi, eat.' **32** But He said to them, 'I have food to eat that you do not know about.' **33** So the disciples were saying to one another, 'No one brought Him anything to eat, did he?' **34** Jesus said to them, 'My food is to do the will of Him who sent Me and to accomplish His work. **35** Do you not say, 'There are yet four months, and then comes the harvest'? Behold, I say to you, lift up your eyes and look on the fields, that they are white for harvest. **36** Already he who reaps is receiving wages and is gathering fruit for life eternal; so that he who sows and he who reaps may rejoice together. **37** For in this case the saying is true, 'One sows and another reaps.' **38** I sent you to reap that for which you have not labored; others have labored and you have entered into their labor.'

39 From that city many of the Samaritans believed in Him because of the word of the woman who testified, 'He told me all the things that I have done.' **40** So when the Samaritans came to Jesus, they were asking Him to stay with them; and He stayed there two days. **41** Many more believed because of His word; **42** and they were saying to the woman, 'It is no longer because of what you said that we believe, for we have heard for ourselves and know that this One is indeed the Savior of the world.'

43 After the two days He went forth from there into Galilee. **44** For Jesus Himself testified that a prophet has no honor in his own country. **45** So when He came to Galilee, the Galileans received Him, having seen all the things that He did in Jerusalem at the feast; for they themselves also went to the feast.

46 Therefore He came again to Cana of Galilee where He had made the water wine. And there was a royal official whose son was sick at Capernaum. **47** When he heard that Jesus had come out of Judea into Galilee, he went to Him and was imploring Him to come down and heal his son; for he was at the point of death. **48** So Jesus said to him, 'Unless you people see signs and wonders, you simply will not believe.' **49** The royal official said to Him, 'Sir, come down before my child dies.' **50** Jesus said to him, 'Go; your son lives.' The man believed the word that Jesus spoke to him and started off. **51** As he was now going down, his slaves met him, saying that his son was living. **52** So he inquired of them the hour when he began to get better. Then they said to him, 'Yesterday at the seventh hour the fever left him.' **53** So the father knew that it was at that hour in which Jesus said to him, 'Your son lives'; and he himself believed and his whole household. **54** This is again a second sign that Jesus performed when He had come out of Judea into Galilee."

1. Who shows up in verse 27?

2. What was the woman's testimony to her community? What was their response to Jesus?

3. In the context of being in Samaria and His encounter at the well, what is Jesus saying to His short-sighted disciples in verses 31–39?

4. How does Jesus respond to this city full of outcasts (v. 40)?

5. What transformation takes place in the village of Sychar in 48 hours? What was the testimony of the Samaritans after two days with Jesus? (vv. 39–42)

6. Where did Jesus go from Sychar (v. 43)? How was He received and why (v. 45)?

7. What is the circumstance in Cana on Jesus' second visit (vv. 46–47)?

NOTE: The distance between Cana and Capernaum is twenty miles, which is the average distance a person could walk in a day, depending on terrain, weather, and time of year. Scholars estimate Jesus walked anywhere from 15,000–21,000 miles while He was on earth.

8. What did the man ask Jesus for? What did Jesus say (v. 48)? What was Jesus saying about the people's faith (see v. 45)?

9. Describe the royal official's progression of faith from verses 47, 50, and 53. Circle the word "believed." How does his faith change and why?

10. Did Jesus do what the father asked Him to do? What is demonstrated about Jesus' healing power in this passage?

11. What affect did this healing have on the official's family? How is the faith seen in verses 47 and 50 different from the faith in verse 53?

12. List the attributes of God seen on display in John 4.

Application

Do you trust God to take care of you even if/when He doesn't do it your way? Is it hard to resist the temptation to take care of your own needs? Learn from the mistakes of our brothers and sisters who've gone before us (see Genesis 16). Pray for unconditional trust and faith in God, our perfect Healer, Provider, and Protector who is always right on time!

STUDY FIVE
Jesus Rejected at Nazareth

The tide turned quickly in this passage, from wonder to rage. Jesus visited His hometown and, not surprisingly, those who knew Him since He was "this big" had a hard time accepting that the carpenter's Son was the fulfillment of Isaiah's prophecy. As the Lord's Anointed, Jesus read aloud Isaiah's words—that He came for the poor and the prisoner, the blind and the brokenhearted. And the hearers marveled with joy. But Jesus knew their heart, and so He dug a little deeper. He shone light on their doubt, illustrated their unfaithfulness, and warned of their rejection. Instead of responding in repentance, His clarifying truth uncovered their contempt. And for now, the opportunity for salvation slips away.

Luke 4:14–30

"**14** And Jesus returned to Galilee in the power of the Spirit, and news about Him spread throughout all the surrounding district. **15** And He began teaching in their synagogues and was praised by all.

16 And He came to Nazareth, where He had been brought up; and as was His custom, He entered the synagogue on the Sabbath, and stood up to read. **17** And the book of the prophet Isaiah was handed to Him. And He opened the book and found the place where it was written,

18 'The Spirit of the Lord is upon Me,

Because He anointed Me to preach the gospel to the poor.

He has sent Me to proclaim release to the captives,

And recovery of sight to the blind,

To set free those who are oppressed,

19 To proclaim the favorable year of the Lord.'

20 And He closed the book, gave it back to the attendant and sat down; and the eyes of all in the synagogue were fixed on Him. **21** And He began to say to them, 'Today this Scripture has been fulfilled in your hearing.' **22** And all were speaking well of Him, and wondering at the gracious words which were falling from His lips; and they were saying, 'Is this not Joseph's son?' **23** And He said to them, 'No doubt you will quote this proverb to Me, 'Physician, heal yourself! Whatever we heard was done at Capernaum, do here in your hometown as well.' **24** And He said, 'Truly I say to you, no prophet is welcome in his hometown. **25** But I say to you in truth, there were many widows in Israel in the days of Elijah, when the sky was shut up for three years and six months, when a great famine came over all the land; **26** and yet Elijah was sent to none of them, but only to Zarephath, in the land of Sidon, to a woman who was a widow. **27** And there were many lepers in Israel in the time of Elisha the prophet; and none of them was cleansed, but only Naaman the Syrian.' **28** And all the people in the synagogue were filled with rage as they heard these things; **29** and they got up and drove Him out of the city, and led Him to the brow of the hill on which their city had been built, in order to throw Him down the cliff. **30** But passing through their midst, He went His way."

1. Where and when does this scene take place?

2. What scroll was Jesus handed? Who selected the passage? Why this passage?

3. How does Jesus describe His ministry using the words of the prophet Isaiah? Why does Jesus stop reading where He does (see Isaiah 61:1–2)?

4. Describe this Sabbath scene and the mood of the Jews from verses 16–17, 20, and 22.

5. What does Jesus proclaim about Himself in verse 21?

6. What does Jesus know about the hearts and expectations of the people? (v. 23)

7. What does Jesus reveal in verses 24–27 about His ministry and purpose and how does this expand on the truth from Isaiah 61? Read 1 Kings 17 and 2 Kings 5:1–14 for context to the stories He references.

8. How did the people respond in verses 28–29?

9. What happened to Jesus?

Application
Do you fall into any of the categories Jesus said He came to deliver? How does this scene encourage you? (Luke 4:18–19)

WRAPPING UP

Isaiah 61:1–2 is the job description of Jesus as the Messiah. In reading the prophecy, Jesus first acknowledged that He was filled with the Spirit, who enabled Him to do what He came to do. Consider: *the Son of God, as a Man, relied on the power of God's Spirit working in Him.* That is an example for us. The Messiah was obedient to and dependent upon the Holy Spirit to lead, guide, and direct every step of His ministry on earth!

In Ephesians 1:15–22, Paul prays for the gracious intervention of the "spirit of wisdom and of revelation in the knowledge of Him" in the church in Ephesus. Take a moment to pray this for yourself and for those you know who need the eyes of their heart enlightened.

~ Map of Jesus in Capernaum ~

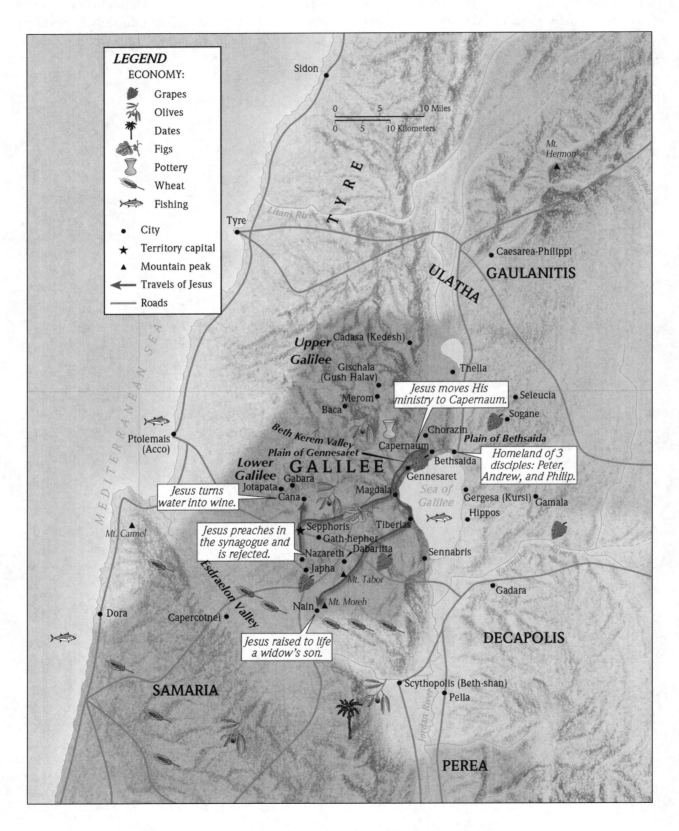

JESUS, THE HEALER

*"When evening came, they brought to Him many who were demon-possessed;
and He cast out the spirits with a word, and healed all who were ill. This was
to fulfill what was spoken through Isaiah the prophet: 'HE HIMSELF TOOK
OUR INFIRMITIES AND CARRIED AWAY OUR DISEASES.'"*
Matthew 8:16–17

magine living with a disease that isolates you from community and fellowship. Imagine being unable to care for yourself, without hope or help. Imagine not feeling the touch of another human being for years.

Now imagine those same conditions on the inside. A soul riddled with the disease of selfishness. The sickness of self-righteousness permeating a heart. Human contact becomes an occasion to inflict pain.

The "sick" in these passages take many forms—leper and demoniac, religious leaders and tax collectors—some more aware of their condition than others. But all in need of healing.

It is compassion that moves Jesus toward those who are hurting. But He knows mankind's deepest need is not to be physically healed but, rather, forgiven and restored to a right relationship with Him. The slate wiped clean. Hearts made whole.

The healing ministry of Jesus drew large crowds, which is not surprising. The purpose of these miracles was to give glory to God; they were also designed to demonstrate the power and deity of Jesus. But His real mission was to call sinners to repentance. And it is there that the real cure is found—in the balm of redemptive grace.

STUDY ONE
The First Disciples and the Galilee Ministry

This week, we will see Jesus in action. He called His first followers: men of the sea by trade—strong, skilled at casting and catching, and familiar with dependence upon the Lord's provision. They responded not to a call to repentance but, rather, to a promise of transformation. As they set out for the surrounding cities and towns, throngs of people began to follow them, drawn by Jesus' gospel message and desperate for their suffering to end. The sick, diseased, afflicted, and possessed, with hearts and bodies broken, were compelled to come. Hope, at last, was here!

Matthew 4:13–25

"**13** . . . and leaving Nazareth, He came and settled in Capernaum, which is by the sea, in the region of Zebulun and Naphtali. **14** This was to fulfill what was spoken through Isaiah the prophet:

15 'The land of Zebulun and the land of Naphtali,
By the way of the sea, beyond the Jordan, Galilee of the Gentiles—
16 'The people who were sitting in darkness saw a great Light,
And those who were sitting in the land and shadow of death,
Upon them a Light dawned.'

17 From that time Jesus began to preach and say, 'Repent, for the kingdom of heaven is at hand.'

18 Now as Jesus was walking by the Sea of Galilee, He saw two brothers, Simon who was called Peter, and Andrew his brother, casting a net into the sea; for they were fishermen. **19** And He said to them, 'Follow Me, and I will make you fishers of men.' **20** Immediately they left their nets and followed Him. **21** Going on from there He saw two other brothers, James the son of Zebedee, and John his brother, in the boat with Zebedee their father, mending their nets; and He called them. **22** Immediately they left the boat and their father, and followed Him.

23 Jesus was going throughout all Galilee, teaching in their synagogues and proclaiming the gospel of the kingdom, and healing every kind of disease and every kind of sickness among the people.

24 The news about Him spread throughout all Syria; and they brought to Him all who were ill, those suffering with various diseases and pains, demoniacs, epileptics, paralytics; and He healed them. **25** Large crowds followed Him from Galilee and the Decapolis and Jerusalem and Judea and from beyond the Jordan."

1. Where did Jesus live? What was the setting of this passage?

2. What was the message of Jesus in verse 17?

3. How was Jesus fulfilling Isaiah's prophecy at this point (verses 15–16)?

4. Who were Jesus' first disciples? Where did Jesus find them? (vv. 18–22)

5. What did Jesus promise to do? What was required of the men He called (vv. 20, 22)?

6. Observe and record what is known about these men.

   What character or personality traits are important for fishermen?

   Read Luke 5:1–11. What do these verses add to the story? What does it say about Jesus' provision for the men who will follow Him?

7. What does verse 23 say Jesus did after calling His disciples? Write down the verbs listed in this verse.

8. Write down the order of events and causes and their effects in verses 23–25.

9. What attributes of God do you see at work and on display in this passage?

Application
How would a life of obscurity be preparation for being a disciple of Jesus? Why do you think He called disciples? What does that say to you about discipleship, fellowship, and the body of Christ? (Genesis 2:18, 2 Timothy 2:2) What in your life has the Lord used to help or equip you to follow Him?

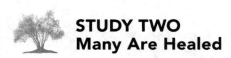 **STUDY TWO**
Many Are Healed

Jesus is Amazing would have to be the headline of "The Jerusalem Times" had there been a newspaper of the day. His teaching was inspiring; His healing powers left them in awe, and, even in rebuke, demons proclaimed Jesus "the Son of God" — perhaps the only truth they had ever spoken. It should be noted that while the evil spirits recognized the Holy One at once, the people of Israel were still puzzling it out. *Who is this Man and what exactly is He talking about?* The Healer of their nation was standing among them, and they did not have eyes to see. Jesus not only healed "all those" who came, He healed His closest friends, too. It would have been awe-inspiring to see Jesus at the bedside of Simon's mother-in-law, easing her suffering with His very words. How could you not be moved to serve this great and gentle Physician?

Luke 4:31–41

"**31** And He came down to Capernaum, a city of Galilee, and He was teaching them on the Sabbath; **32** and they were amazed at His teaching, for His message was with authority. **33** In the synagogue there was a man possessed by the spirit of an unclean demon, and he cried out with a loud voice, **34** 'Let us alone! What business do we have with each other, Jesus of Nazareth? Have You come to destroy us? I know who You are—the Holy One of God!' **35** But Jesus rebuked him, saying, 'Be quiet and come out of him!' And when the demon had thrown him down in the midst of the people, he came out of him without doing him any harm. **36** And amazement came upon them all, and they began talking with one another saying, 'What is this message? For with authority and power He commands the unclean spirits and they come out.' **37** And the report about Him was spreading into every locality in the surrounding district.

38 Then He got up and left the synagogue, and entered Simon's home. Now Simon's mother-in-law was suffering from a high fever, and they asked Him to help her. **39** And standing over her, He rebuked the fever, and it left her; and she immediately got up and waited on them.

40 While the sun was setting, all those who had any who were sick with various diseases brought them to Him; and laying His hands on each one of them, He was healing them. **41** Demons also were coming out of many, shouting, 'You are the Son of God!' But rebuking them, He would not allow them to speak, because they knew Him to be the Christ."

1. Where is Jesus now in the story?

2. What was Jesus doing in verses 31–32? How did the people respond? Why might they have felt this way?

3. Who was in the synagogue that might have been unexpected?

4. What did this man say to Jesus? What did he say about Jesus?

5. What two commands did Jesus give?

6. What happened next? How did the people respond?

7. The scenery shifts in this passage, moving us from the synagogue to Simon's home. Who was Simon? (John 1:42)

8. Who was sick? What does this tell us about Simon?

9. How did Jesus respond?

10. How did she respond? What does this tell us?

11. Why is the time of day important in verse 40?

NOTE: The Jewish Sabbath is approximately twenty-five hours long, officially beginning at sunset on Friday and lasting until about an hour after sunset on Saturday.

12. How is Jesus' compassion seen in this portion of scripture? (v. 40)

13. Compare the response of the people seen in previous passages (Luke 4:28–30) to the proclamations of the demons who encounter Jesus. What is significant about this?

14. How is Jesus fulfilling the prophecy in Isaiah 61:1 in these passages?

Application
When was the last time you were amazed by Jesus?

STUDY THREE
The Leper in Galilee

Everyone was looking for Jesus, but so far, no one actually saw Him. The people were intrigued by His teaching and drawn to His healing powers, but the message of each miracle had yet to penetrate their hearts. The leper in this passage had faith in Jesus' ability to heal him, but he did not appear to have faith in Jesus as Savior. Had he realized Who Jesus was, he might have obeyed His directive and adhered to the law (Leviticus 14:1–32). Perhaps that is why Jesus began His day in the presence of His Father. While His divine power—no matter how often He used it—never diminished, His flesh was weak, and He knew it. Prayer was a source of strength. In His wisdom and need as a human Man, Jesus realized communion with God was essential to His endurance. And there would be much yet to endure.

Mark 1:35–45
"**35** In the early morning, while it was still dark, Jesus got up, left the house, and went away to a secluded place, and was praying there. **36** Simon and his companions searched for Him; **37** they found Him, and said to Him, 'Everyone is looking for You.' **38** He said to them, 'Let us go somewhere else to the towns nearby, so that I may preach there also; for that is what I came for.' **39** And He went into their synagogues throughout all Galilee, preaching and casting out the demons.

40 And a leper came to Jesus, beseeching Him and falling on his knees before Him, and saying, 'If You are willing, You can make me clean.' **41** Moved with compassion, Jesus stretched out His hand and touched him, and said to him, 'I am willing; be cleansed.' **42** Immediately the leprosy left him and he was cleansed. **43** And He sternly warned him and immediately sent him away, **44** and He said to him, 'See that you say nothing to anyone; but go, show yourself to the priest and offer for your cleansing what Moses commanded, as a testimony to them.' **45** But he went out and began to proclaim it freely and to spread the news around, to such an extent that Jesus could no longer publicly enter a city, but stayed out in unpopulated areas; and they were coming to Him from everywhere."

1. How does verse 35 describe Jesus' prayer life? Observe and write down the verbs used.

2. Contrast Jesus' and Simon Peter's approach to ministry implied in verses 35–37. What was different about their perspectives on Jesus' primary mission on earth?

3. Why was everyone looking for Jesus?

4. What does Jesus do? Why? (v. 38)

5. Who appears on the scene in verse 40 and what does he do and say? What does this say about the man's faith?

6. Read Leviticus 13:45–46. What does Old Testament Scripture say about lepers?

7. Observe and describe Jesus' response to this man and His instructions in verses 43–44. What was the greater purpose in Jesus' command to the healed leper to show himself to the priest (v. 44)?

8. Why do you think the healed man disobeyed Jesus in verse 45? What was the effect?

9. What attributes of God do you see in Jesus in this encounter?

Application

We read many times in the Bible that the word about Jesus spread quickly and throughout the region. This was a time long before social media, yet we know from experience that good—and bad—news travels fast. How have you seen social media used for good—even to spread the Gospel of Jesus—in your community and the world?

STUDY FOUR
The Paralytic in Capernaum

A packed house. Standing room only. Elbow-to-elbow. This kind of expectant crowd was commonplace wherever Jesus went. What was also common was the disconnect between Jesus' mission and the people's motives. Jesus was there to teach Truth; the people came for relief. They were focused on alleviating their physical suffering and, in compassion, Jesus healed. But the sickness He was most concerned about was a spiritual one. Inserted into this story of friendship, faith, and forgiveness, we see a progressive and degenerative condition in the hearts of the cynical scribes. They were hardened by pride and infected beyond moral remedy. And for this disease, the love of Jesus is the only cure.

Mark 2:1–12

"When He had come back to Capernaum several days afterward, it was heard that He was at home. **2** And many were gathered together, so that there was no longer room, not even near the door; and He was speaking the word to them. **3** And they came, bringing to Him a paralytic, carried by four men. **4** Being unable to get to Him because of the crowd, they removed the roof above Him; and when they had dug an opening, they let down the pallet on which the paralytic was lying. **5** And Jesus seeing their faith said to the paralytic, 'Son, your sins are forgiven.' **6** But some of the scribes were sitting there and reasoning in their hearts, **7** 'Why does this man speak that way? He is blaspheming; who can forgive sins but God alone?' **8** Immediately Jesus, aware in His spirit that they were reasoning that way within themselves, said to them, 'Why are you reasoning about these things in your hearts? **9** Which is easier, to say to the paralytic, 'Your sins are forgiven'; or to say, 'Get up, and pick up your pallet and walk'? **10** But so that you may know that the Son of Man has authority on earth to forgive sins'—He said to the paralytic, **11** 'I say to you, get up, pick up your pallet and go home.' **12** And he got up and immediately picked up the pallet and went out in the sight of everyone, so that they were all amazed and were glorifying God, saying, 'We have never seen anything like this.'"

1. Describe the scene in Mark 2:1–2: who, what, where, when, and why?

2. Who shows up in the scene in verse 3? What do they do in verse 4?

3. What does Jesus see and say in verse 5? Why might He have said this?

4. Observe and record opposition to Jesus and His response to it in the story. (See also Luke 5:17)

5. Record the evidence of Jesus' deity in verses 5–11.

6. What are Jesus' commands in verse 11? What happens in verse 12?

Application

The paralytic had great friends who brought him to Jesus. What kind of friend are you? Are you the type of friend who brings others to Jesus? Who in your life is in need of the Great Physician and what can you do to introduce others to Him?

STUDY FIVE
The Call of Levi (Matthew)

Just as Jesus' healing of the paralytic was motivated by compassion, so was His call of Levi. Tax collectors were greedy swindlers, cheats by reputation, so to be called into relationship with anyone—especially Jesus Himself—was an act of pure grace. The religious leaders missed the point once again, taking Jesus to task for associating with sinners like Levi and his peers. Turning their religion on its head, Jesus wasted no words in explaining His purpose: *I came for sinners just like this man, He told them. I heal, but in a much deeper way than you even realize you need. This man left his old life behind, trusting me in faith. You cling to self-sufficiency and self-righteousness. The sickness in your souls is the real thief, robbing you of life and stealing your joy.*

Luke 5:27–32

"**27** After that He went out and noticed a tax collector named Levi sitting in the tax booth, and He said to him, 'Follow Me.' **28** And he left everything behind, and got up and began to follow Him.

29 And Levi gave a big reception for Him in his house; and there was a great crowd of tax collectors and other people who were reclining at the table with them. **30** The Pharisees and their scribes began grumbling at His disciples, saying, 'Why do you eat and drink with the tax collectors and sinners?' **31** And Jesus answered and said to them, 'It is not those who are well who need a physician, but those who are sick. **32** I have not come to call the righteous but sinners to repentance.'"

NOTE: See also Matthew 9:9–13

1. Where does Jesus find His next disciple? What names is he known by? What is known from Scripture and history about his profession? (Use the dictionary at biblestudytools.com and research "publican" or "tax.")

2. How does Levi respond to Jesus' invitation? What is the first thing he does after that?

3. Who attended Levi's party? Who is the party for?

4. How did the Pharisees and scribes respond to the gathering? Why do you think they felt that way?

5. What distinction did Jesus make for them?

6. Review and list the people who were healed in this week's study. From what were they healed? What was their presenting need? What was their greatest need?

Application

Is there an example for us to follow in these six verses? Is there a warning for us to heed in these verses? Where do you see joy in this passage? How is God speaking to you through this story?

WRAPPING UP

There would be no need of physicians without those who are sick. Jesus makes this point about Himself many times. He is the Great Physician of the soul because our souls are in great need of healing. We are His patients, and sin is our disease.

There are no "small" or lesser sins. We are natural-born enemies of God (Romans 5:10, Colossians 1:21), and every sin separates us from Him. Sin is, in fact, fatal, and there is but one remedy: Jesus. His death on the cross and resurrection to life has forever removed us from the grip of death and grants us eternal life. We are healed, from the inside out!

We saw this week that Jesus Himself came to His Father's throne of grace before He ministered to the masses. Remember the power of prayer as you reach out to those you wish to introduce to Jesus. The disabled, downtrodden, disappointed, disenfranchised—ask the Lord to give you compassion for those in need, and for persistent endurance and courageous faith to bring them to the Savior.

—This is likely the end of Jesus' first year of ministry.

Notes

JESUS, EQUAL TO GOD

"But He answered them, 'My Father is working until now, and I Myself am working.' For this reason therefore the Jews were seeking all the more to kill Him, because He not only was breaking the Sabbath, but also was calling God His own Father, making Himself equal with God."
JOHN 5:17–18

Claiming to be equal to God is something most people today associate with mental illness. Bad things have happened to people who follow those who claim to be "God." That's because they are deceivers. They are not equal to God because the only One who was and is, now sits at the right hand of the Father—His Son and our Savior, Jesus Christ.

Putting ourselves in the shoes of the ancient Israelites, it's easier to understand why they struggled to believe Jesus was God made flesh. Jesus didn't meet their expectations. He wasn't a warrior or political leader intent on overthrowing the government and making the nation of Israel the center of the world. He was a carpenter's son from nowhere. His earthly life began in scandal. His followers consisted mostly of fishermen, a tax collector, and common men who didn't really believe everything they heard Jesus say anyway.

And it was this claim—"I and the Father are one." (John 10:30)—more than anything else Jesus said or did that fueled the religious leaders' determination to put Him to death.

This is a difficult concept for us to grasp as well. Jesus as God *and* God's Son is a mind-blowing truth. John 1:1 addresses this in a way that is at once simple and astounding: from before time began, Jesus was with God, and at the same time, Jesus was God.

The passages for this week are important because, in them, Jesus provides proof of His relationship to God. Jesus speaks of four witnesses to His equality with God, and while His arguments are complex and tight, His message is simple and clear: *hear, believe, and receive. Come to me and have life.*

This message is evidence and an invitation to those who heard Jesus speak and to those who read His words today. Pray for the faith to believe what is hard to understand, and for a heart filled with love for the One who is beyond our comprehension.

STUDY ONE
The Healing at Bethesda

A multitude of very sick people gathered by a supposed healing pool in Jerusalem, and that's where "Jesus saw him"—one man, lying among the many. Jesus healed him with just a word, a command to get up, carry his mat, and walk. Atrophied muscles and weakened bones were instantly made new. Jesus' act of grace set controversy in motion. The Pharisees accuse the healed man of breaking Sabbath law, and the man points them to Jesus. Jesus then took the opportunity to make a divine and radical claim: *Yes, I did "work" on the Sabbath, just like my Father. He doesn't refrain from showing mercy and grace on the Sabbath day, and neither do I.* Here was Jesus' first proclamation of deity—He is one with God in activity and essence.

John 5:1–17

"After these things there was a feast of the Jews, and Jesus went up to Jerusalem. **2** Now there is in Jerusalem by the sheep gate a pool, which is called in Hebrew Bethesda, having five porticoes. **3** In these lay a multitude of those who were sick, blind, lame, and withered, [waiting for the moving of the waters; **4** for an angel of the Lord went down at certain seasons into the pool and stirred up the water; whoever then first, after the stirring up of the water, stepped in was made well from whatever disease with which he was afflicted.] **5** A man was there who had been ill for thirty-eight years. **6** When Jesus saw him lying there, and knew that he had already been a long time in that condition, He said to him, 'Do you wish to get well?' **7** The sick man answered Him, 'Sir, I have no man to put me into the pool when the water is stirred up, but while I am coming, another steps down before me.' **8** Jesus said to him, 'Get up, pick up your pallet and walk.' **9** Immediately the man became well, and picked up his pallet and began to walk.

Now it was the Sabbath on that day. **10** So the Jews were saying to the man who was cured, 'It is the Sabbath, and it is not permissible for you to carry your pallet.' **11** But he answered them, 'He who made me well was the one who said to me, 'Pick up your pallet and walk.' **12** They asked him, 'Who is the man who said to you, 'Pick up your pallet and walk'?' **13** But the man who was healed did not know who it was, for Jesus had slipped away while there was a crowd in that place. **14** Afterward Jesus found him in the temple and said to him, 'Behold, you have become well; do not sin anymore, so that nothing worse happens to you.' **15** The man went away, and told the Jews that it was Jesus who had made him well. **16** For this reason the Jews were persecuting Jesus, because He was doing these things on the Sabbath. **17** But He answered them, 'My Father is working until now, and I Myself am working.'"

1. What is the setting of this scene (vv. 1-3)?

NOTE: The word "multitude" is used throughout Scripture and defined as a mass of ordinary people without power or influence.

2. Use biblestudytools.com and research the meaning of the word "Bethesda." How does understanding the name enhance your understanding of the passage?

3. How many were at the pool? Who did Jesus see at the pool and what do we know about him?

4. What did Jesus say to the man? Why would He ask that question? How did the man respond? Can any conclusions be drawn about this man from his response?

5. The end of verse 9 gives a clue to upcoming conflict. Describe the power struggle between Jesus and the Jews. What does the law say about the Sabbath in Exodus 20: 8–11?

6. What does verse 10 of John reveal was the priority of the Jews at that time?

7. What did the man know about Who healed him (vv. 11–13)?

8. What happened next in verse 14? What does this verse reveal was Jesus' main concern? What does it reveal about the healed man? (see James 5:15–16)

9. What is the reason given in verse 16 of John for the Jews' persecution of Jesus? Why would Jesus' actions be threatening to them?

Application

It is challenging to see that, out of the multitude of invalids, Jesus healed just one. Isaiah 55:9 reminds us that God's ways are higher and better than ours, yet we struggle when life doesn't make sense. What comfort does God's sovereignty give you? How does Revelation 21:4–5 give you hope?

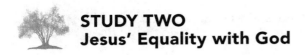

STUDY TWO
Jesus' Equality with God

Jesus clearly aligned Himself with God in this passage, calling Himself "Son" and, at the same time, claiming to be God in every way. Jesus said He does nothing without looking to the Father first, acknowledging intentional and voluntary submission to God's will. Jesus described the different roles of God the Father and Jesus the Son—equal in importance and honor, and distinct in function. This is where we tend to nod off, when the discussion takes a theological turn. So stop and pray for fresh ears, like the first-century hearers: Jesus was the most captivating teacher and compassionate leader the world had ever known, and His claims were startling! God as "Father" was a radical idea to the Jews, and even more the notion that He would humbly dwell with them as a Man. Was this blasphemy, a crime deserving death? Or could He be the Promised One, who had come to remove their guilt and shame with the offer of new life?

John 5:18–29

"**18** For this reason therefore the Jews were seeking all the more to kill Him, because He not only was breaking the Sabbath, but also was calling God His own Father, making Himself equal with God.

19 Therefore Jesus answered and was saying to them, 'Truly, truly, I say to you, the Son can do nothing of Himself, unless it is something He sees the Father doing; for whatever the Father does, these things the Son also does in like manner. **20** For the Father loves the Son, and shows Him all things that He Himself is doing; and the Father will show Him greater works than these, so that you will marvel. **21** For just as the Father raises the dead and gives them life, even so the Son also gives life to whom He wishes. **22** For not even the Father judges anyone, but He has given all judgment to the Son, **23** so that all will honor the Son even as they honor the Father. He who does not honor the Son does not honor the Father who sent Him.

24 'Truly, truly, I say to you, he who hears My word, and believes Him who sent Me, has eternal life, and does not come into judgment, but has passed out of death into life.

25 Truly, truly, I say to you, an hour is coming and now is, when the dead will hear the voice of the Son of God, and those who hear will live. **26** For just as the Father has life in Himself, even so He gave to the Son also to have life in Himself; **27** and He gave Him authority to execute judgment, because He is the Son of Man. **28** Do not marvel at this; for an hour is coming, in which all who are in the tombs will hear His voice, **29** and will come forth; those who did the good deeds to a resurrection of life, those who committed the evil deeds to a resurrection of judgment.'"

1. Verse 18 expands on the Jews' feelings toward Jesus. What was stirring up the Jews?

2. Look up the word "Sabbath" (Simply "Google" the word or try the dictionary resources found on biblestudytools.com for a deeper study). Now read Genesis 2:2–3. Who created the Sabbath and for what purpose? Were the Pharisees right in their accusation? Why or why not?

3. How does Jesus describe the Father-Son relationship? (vv. 19–21) What does verse 20 say is the root of the Father and Son relationship?

4. How does Jesus say He is equal to God? How does He say He is distinct from God?

5. How does Jesus describe His role as Judge? (vv. 22–23, 27)

6. Who does Jesus say will be resurrected and live forever? What determines what they are resurrected "to?" (vv. 24, 28–29)

Application

In this passage and many others, Jesus was accused of breaking the Sabbath. Yet we know the original purpose of the Sabbath was not about keeping a list of rules, but to point us to the worship of our Provider. We can rest because we trust Him! How well do you rest? What does it look like? If you do not observe a "Sabbath" at any time of the week, month, or year, what can you do to purposefully rest and focus on the good gifts of God?

A DEEPER LOOK

Use a dictionary and define the word *legalism* (or for a deeper explanation, visit biblestudytools.com and use their dictionary resources). In this story, beginning in John 5:1, we see how their strict adherence to the rules blinds the religious leaders to the needs around them. Ask the Holy Spirit to search your heart and life: Can you remember a time when you prioritized rules over relationship? Or "right" behavior over compassion and grace?

Read the verses below and observe what Scripture says about mercy. Write down the truths that instruct or encourage you. Pray for mercy to be the "rule" in your life.

Psalms 18:25

James 2:12–13

Psalms 25:6–9

1 Peter 2:10

Matthew 5:7

Jude 1:22–23

Luke 6:36

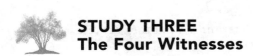

STUDY THREE
The Four Witnesses

At this point, the miracle of the healed invalid was all but forgotten in light of Jesus' remarkable discourse. This was the first time Jesus declared at length and in depth who He was—the whole truth and nothing but. And like a wise litigator, Jesus presented four witnesses to His case. Not because He thought He must convince the world of who He was; His witnesses are for us, those of little faith and short memory. In verse 31, Jesus said He knew He would not be believed if He was the only One to give testimony to His deity. So, in Christ's courtroom, character witnesses emerge: His forerunner John, His miraculous works, His glorious Father, and the trustworthiness of Scripture. In spite of all the evidence, the Pharisees remained faithless—unable to hear, see, receive, or love.

John 5:30–47
"**30** "I can do nothing on My own initiative. As I hear, I judge; and My judgment is just, because I do not seek My own will, but the will of Him who sent Me.
31 "If I alone testify about Myself, My testimony is not true. **32** There is another who testifies of Me, and I know that the testimony which He gives about Me is true.

Witness of John
33 You have sent to John, and he has testified to the truth. **34** But the testimony which I receive is not from man, but I say these things so that you may be saved. **35** He was the lamp that was burning and was shining and you were willing to rejoice for a while in his light.

Witness of Works

36 But the testimony which I have is greater than the testimony of John; for the works which the Father has given Me to accomplish—the very works that I do—testify about Me, that the Father has sent Me.

Witness of the Father

37 And the Father who sent Me, He has testified of Me. You have neither heard His voice at any time nor seen His form. 38 You do not have His word abiding in you, for you do not believe Him whom He sent.

Witness of the Scripture

39 You search the Scriptures because you think that in them you have eternal life; it is these that testify about Me; **40** and you are unwilling to come to Me so that you may have life. **41** I do not receive glory from men; **42** but I know you, that you do not have the love of God in yourselves. **43** I have come in My Father's name, and you do not receive Me; if another comes in his own name, you will receive him. **44** How can you believe, when you receive glory from one another and you do not seek the glory that is from the one and only God? **45** Do not think that I will accuse you before the Father; the one who accuses you is Moses, in whom you have set your hope. **46** For if you believed Moses, you would believe Me, for he wrote about Me. **47** But if you do not believe his writings, how will you believe My words?'"

1. What makes the judgment of Jesus just? (v. 30)

2. How does Jesus describe John (v. 35)?

3. What do the works of Jesus say about Jesus (v. 36)?

4. What does Jesus say keeps the religious leaders from believing the testimony from the Father about Jesus? (vv. 37–38)

5. What does Jesus say is the difference between what the Jews think results in eternal life (v. 39) and what Jesus says gives eternal life (v. 40)?

6. What indictments does Jesus deliver against the Pharisees in verses 40–45?

7. Read Moses' words about Jesus in Deuteronomy 18:15–19. What does Moses reveal about God's plan?

8. What sort of Messiah does Jesus say the Jews will accept (verse 43)?

Application

Do you live your life as though you believe the words of Jesus? How does your belief (or lack of) make a difference in your life and the lives of others?

A DEEPER LOOK

1 John 5:9–12 is another place in Scripture that talks about the testimony of Christ about Himself. Verse 10 says we have proof that we belong to God, a gift the Pharisees in the passages above did not have. Romans 8:16 refers to the same promise.

What is the "testimony" or gift we are given as believers?

You may not remember a "moment" in time where you received Jesus as your Savior, but that definitive memory is not required for salvation. Read the verses below and record the different ways we can have assurance of our salvation in Christ Jesus.

Romans 5:1   Colossians 3:1–4

Romans 8:1, 38–39   Hebrews 7:25

2 Corinthians 13:5   Titus 3:4–7

Philippians 3:8–9

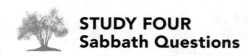 **STUDY FOUR**
Sabbath Questions

In our mind's eye, we can see Jesus and His friends taking a leisurely stroll through a caramel-colored field of wheat. The sun is high, a soft breeze blows. Suddenly, accusing voices pierce the peace of their communion. "We're watching you," the Pharisees sneered. "And you're breaking the law!" Wouldn't these agitators be guilty of the same thing, as they labored to entrap Jesus? As One equal to God, Jesus skillfully cut through their arrogance, reminding them of the Scripture they claimed to be so familiar with: Have you ever heard of David and his hungry men? Or seen in the Law how priests work on the Sabbath? In their eagerness to condemn, the Pharisees neglected what the Lord most desires: compassion. The One who is greater than the Law that they are trying to protect, and the temple where they pretend to worship was standing right before them. But their eyes and hearts were closed.

Matthew 12:1–8
"At that time Jesus went through the grainfields on the Sabbath, and His disciples became hungry and began to pick the heads of grain and eat. **2** But when the Pharisees saw this, they said to Him, 'Look, Your disciples do what is not lawful to do on a Sabbath.' **3** But He said to them, 'Have you not read what David did when he became hungry, he and his companions, **4** how he entered the house of God, and they ate the consecrated bread, which was not lawful for him to eat nor for those with him, but for the priests alone? **5** Or have you not read in the Law, that on the Sabbath the priests in the temple break the Sabbath and are innocent? **6** But I say to you that something greater than the temple is here. **7** But if you had known what this means, 'I desire compassion, and not a sacrifice,' you would not have condemned the innocent.
   8 For the Son of Man is Lord of the Sabbath.'"

1. What day is it? Who are the characters in this scene? What is taking place?

From Dave Guzik's *Commentary on the Bible*: "At this time, many rabbis filled Judaism with elaborate rituals related to the Sabbath and observance of other laws. Ancient rabbis taught that on the Sabbath a man could not carry something in his right hand or in his left hand, across his chest or on his shoulder; but he could carry something with the back of his hand, with his foot, elbow, or in the ear, on the hair, in the hem of his shirt, or in his shoe or sandal."

2. What is the Pharisees accusation? Were they correct? (See Deuteronomy 23:25).

3. Paraphrase the questions Jesus asks. What point is He trying to make?

4. How does this scene connect to Jesus' words in the previous chapter, Matthew 11:28–29?

5. What does verse 7 say the Father desires? What does verse 7 tell us about what the Pharisees valued?

6. What two things does Jesus say He is "over" or "greater than" in this passage? (vv. 6, 8) How does Jesus' position over the institutions He speaks of topple the Pharisees argument?

7. There is precedent in the history of Israel in Scripture for grace outside the bounds of the Law. Read 2 Chronicles 30:17–20 and apply and contrast that principle to the way the Pharisees believed life should be lived.

Application

Compassion can look different depending on the circumstances. Describe a time when you were shown compassion, perhaps undeserved, or demonstrated compassion when it was difficult for you.

STUDY FIVE
Healing on the Sabbath and Choosing the Twelve

Darkness has been hovering in the corners of these accounts in Scripture, and in this passage, it enters boldly, invading hearts and corrupting motives of Israel's so-called spiritual leaders. In the past, the Pharisees had simply been vigilant—looking for Jesus to misstep so that they could find fault. But here, they set Him up. These religious men put the Messiah to the test and prayed that He would fail. Their plan? Accusation, conspiracy, and destruction. Their hardness grieved Jesus, yet His perfect mercy for those in need was unmoved. In the midst of this trial, Jesus continues His ministry. Then He wisely retreats from the frantic pace of life to gather His friends and appoint them His followers. Persecution is beginning, but the Light still shines and continues to grow as ordinary men are called to an extraordinary mission.

Mark 3:1–19

"He entered again into a synagogue; and a man was there whose hand was withered. **2** They were watching Him to see if He would heal him on the Sabbath, so that they might accuse Him. **3** He said to the man with the withered hand, 'Get up and come forward!' **4** And He said to them, 'Is it lawful to do good or to do harm on the Sabbath, to save a life or to kill?' But they kept silent. **5** After looking around at them with anger, grieved at their hardness of heart, He said to the man, 'Stretch out your hand.' And he stretched it out, and his hand was restored. **6** The Pharisees went out and immediately began conspiring with the Herodians against Him, as to how they might destroy Him.

7 Jesus withdrew to the sea with His disciples; and a great multitude from Galilee followed; and also from Judea, **8** and from Jerusalem, and from Idumea, and beyond the Jordan, and the vicinity of Tyre and Sidon, a great number of people heard of all that He was doing and came to Him. **9** And He told His disciples that a boat should stand ready for Him because of the crowd, so that they would not crowd Him; **10** for He had healed many, with the result that all those who had afflictions pressed around Him in order to touch Him. **11** Whenever the unclean spirits saw Him, they would fall down before Him and shout, 'You are the Son of God!' **12** And He earnestly warned them not to tell who He was.

13 And He went up on the mountain and summoned those whom He Himself wanted, and they came to Him. **14** And He appointed twelve, so that they would be with Him and that He could send them out to preach, **15** and to have authority to cast out the demons. **16** And He appointed the twelve: Simon (to whom He gave the name Peter), **17** and James, the son of Zebedee, and John the brother of James (to them He gave the name Boanerges, which means, 'Sons of Thunder'); **18** and Andrew, and Philip, and Bartholomew, and Matthew, and Thomas, and James the son of Alphaeus, and Thaddaeus, and Simon the Zealot; **19** and Judas Iscariot, who betrayed Him."

1. Who is in this scene in verses 1–6? Where and when is it taking place?

2. Why were "they" watching Jesus? Why do you think the man with the withered hand was in the synagogue?

3. How do verses 1–6 describe Jesus?

   a. What did He say?

   b. What did He do?

   c. How did He feel?

4. How do these verses describe the Pharisees?

   a. What did they say?

   b. What did they do?

   c. How did they feel?

5. Summarize the contrasts between Jesus and the Pharisees.

6. Read back through Mark 2 and note the reasons for the Jews' hardened hearts. List your observations below.

7. What happened when Jesus withdrew to the sea in verse 7?

8. Why did the crowd follow Him? Record details from Scripture about the intensity of Jesus' ministry (vv. 9–10).

9. Who was proclaiming Jesus as the Son of God?

10. How did Jesus choose His disciples (see also Luke 6:12–13)?

11. What was the mission of the disciples? (vv. 14–15)

12. List their names. Write down any biographical information you know from Scripture about each man. See also John 1:35–51.

Application

Consider the people who are in your closest circle. What kind of people do you surround yourself with? How would you describe their character? How do you mutually encourage and challenge each other? How do these friends point you to truth and spur you on in your relationship with Jesus?

WRAPPING UP

Jesus spoke some of the most controversial words ever heard in these passages as He proclaimed and proved Himself to be equal to God. The way in which people responded to this truth ranged from disbelief to denial to devising plans to destroy Him.

So what about you? Do you believe what Jesus said about Himself—that He is not just a teacher or a good man, but the Son of God? And not just an obedient, loving Son but at the same time, God Himself? This is truth that should not only be wholly accepted; it must completely transform our lives!

Notes

JESUS, TEACHER OF RIGHTEOUSNESS

"When Jesus saw the crowds, He went up on the mountain; and after He sat down, His disciples came to Him. He opened His mouth and began to teach them . . ."
MATTHEW 5:1–2

Regardless of their stance on His deity, most everyone in the world agrees Jesus was a great Teacher. The Jews of His day — and even to this day — call Him "Rabbi," a term of respect that literally means, "Master," "My great one," and "Teacher."

These three chapters in Matthew contain some of the most familiar words in Scripture and will reveal the true genius of Jesus as Teacher. Blessed are the persecuted, poor in spirit, and pure in heart. Let your light shine before men. Turn the other cheek. Seek and you will find. Don't throw pearls to swine. Your kingdom come.

At the same time, Jesus seemed to be outlining a life that is impossible to live: You must be even more righteous than the most religious among you. Angry, lustful, greedy thoughts in your heart are the same as committing the sin. Forgive the unforgiveable. Love the unlovable. Don't worry. Be perfect.

Jesus turned religion on its head and shattered the expectations of everyone within earshot. This master Teacher raised the standard of living to impossible heights. He stripped away the hypocrisy the religious leaders had been propping themselves up with for centuries, leaving them with nothing—nothing but Himself. Which is exactly the point.

Join Jesus and His disciples as He preaches His great sermon on the hillside, and pray for ears to hear and a heart drawn into a deeper obedience of the One who supplies all we need.

STUDY ONE
The Beatitudes

Familiar with the press of the crowd, Jesus sought a wide space when the multitude started to gather. Jesus was a Man with purpose in all He did, and this day, on a high hill under the open sky, He taught. This was not a typical Jewish lecture about obeying rules and following Moses. Jesus wasn't looking to inspire better behavior. He spoke to those who believed—or desperately wanted to—that there was more to life as they knew it. The Law and its teachers had enslaved them for generations with controlling restrictions. The Law was delivered for the good of Israel, but pouring it over depraved hearts and fleshly desires was like spiritual oil and water, creating a suffocating mixture that yielded death. They were left with a bleak choice: legalism or hopelessness. It is into this distress that Jesus spoke His life-giving words, proclaiming Himself the promised fulfillment.

Matthew 5:1–20

"When Jesus saw the crowds, He went up on the mountain; and after He sat down, His disciples came to Him. **2** He opened His mouth and began to teach them, saying,

3 'Blessed are the poor in spirit, for theirs is the kingdom of heaven.

4 'Blessed are those who mourn, for they shall be comforted.

5 'Blessed are the gentle, for they shall inherit the earth.

6 'Blessed are those who hunger and thirst for righteousness, for they shall be satisfied.

7 'Blessed are the merciful, for they shall receive mercy.

8 'Blessed are the pure in heart, for they shall see God.

9 'Blessed are the peacemakers, for they shall be called sons of God.

10 'Blessed are those who have been persecuted for the sake of righteousness, for theirs is the kingdom of heaven.

11 'Blessed are you when people insult you and persecute you, and falsely say all kinds of evil against you because of Me. **12** Rejoice and be glad, for your reward in heaven is great; for in the same way they persecuted the prophets who were before you.

13 'You are the salt of the earth; but if the salt has become tasteless, how can it be made salty again? It is no longer good for anything, except to be thrown out and trampled under foot by men.

14 'You are the light of the world. A city set on a hill cannot be hidden; **15** nor does anyone light a lamp and put it under a basket, but on the lampstand, and it gives light to all who are in the house. **16** Let your light shine before men in such a way that they may see your good works, and glorify your Father who is in heaven.

17 'Do not think that I came to abolish the Law or the Prophets; I did not come to abolish but to fulfill. **18** For truly I say to you, until heaven and earth pass away, not the smallest letter or stroke shall pass from the Law until all is accomplished. **19** Whoever then annuls one of the least of these commandments, and teaches others to do the same, shall be called least in the kingdom of heaven; but whoever keeps and teaches them, he shall be called great in the kingdom of heaven.

20 'For I say to you that unless your righteousness surpasses that of the scribes and Pharisees, you will not enter the kingdom of heaven.'"

1. Who is in this scene in verse 1? Where does it take place? Based on previous descriptions of the people following Jesus, what specific groups might have been a part of this scene? Who is Jesus specifically teaching?

2. Verses 3–12 are known as the Beatitudes. Look up "beatitudes" in a Bible dictionary (see biblestudy-tools.com) and record what you discover. What is the big idea of what Jesus is teaching in these verses? How is this different from the Law the Jews had been taught all their lives?

3. Make a list of the heart attitudes that Jesus says will be blessed. What are the blessings?

4. What does Jesus call His followers in verses 13–14?

5. What commands does Jesus give or imply in verses 13–16?

6. What is the "light" that men are to see in verse 16? Why does Jesus call the people to let their light shine before men? What should be the response of men to seeing the good works of believers?

7. What is the promise made in verses 17–18? What warnings are given in verses 19–20?

8. Read Galatians 3:21–26. How do these verses help explain what Jesus says in verse 17?

9. Read Ezekiel 36:25–27. In light of this promise from the Lord through His prophet, how is it possible for "your righteousness (to surpass) that of the scribes and Pharisees" (v. 20)? How do the words from Ezekiel connect to what Jesus says His purpose is in verse 17?

Application

"The first sixteen verses of Matthew 5 describe the true Christian and deal with character. The rest of the Sermon on the Mount deals with conduct that grows out of character. Character always comes before conduct, because what we are determines what we do." (from *Weirsbe's Expository Outlines on the New Testament* by Dr. Warren Weirsbe)

How does this statement help you understand Jesus' teaching?

STUDY TWO
Personal Relationships

Imagine the teachings of the scribes and Pharisees as a tangled ball of string. Here, Jesus unwinds their words one thread at a time. You've been told, Jesus said, that behavior is the measuring rod for righteousness. But I'm saying it goes much deeper than that. Whatever the relationship, your heart matters most. Your personal holiness exceeds the righteousness of the religious only when humility is the highest pursuit. Reconciliation and redemption, loss and love, are the bywords of abundant life. The heart rails against this call to vulnerability and sacrifice while at the same time, longing to give and receive the free grace of Jesus. To the hearers of the day, Jesus was turning the world upside down. But in light of eternity, Jesus was speaking of life as it was always meant to be.

Matthew 5:21–48

"**21** 'You have heard that the ancients were told, 'You shall not commit murder' and 'Whoever commits murder shall be liable to the court.' **22** But I say to you that everyone who is angry with his brother shall be guilty before the court; and whoever says to his brother, 'You good-for-nothing,' shall be guilty before the supreme court; and whoever says, 'You fool,' shall be guilty enough to go into the fiery hell. **23** Therefore if you are presenting your offering at the altar, and there remember that your brother has something against you, **24** leave your offering there before the altar and go; first be reconciled to your brother, and then come and present your offering. **25** Make friends quickly with your opponent at law while you are with him on the way, so that your opponent may not hand you over to the judge, and the judge to the officer, and you be thrown into prison. **26** Truly I say to you, you will not come out of there until you have paid up the last cent.

27 'You have heard that it was said, 'You shall not commit adultery'; **28** but I say to you that everyone who looks at a woman with lust for her has already committed adultery with her in his heart. **29** If your right eye makes you stumble, tear it out and throw it from you; for it is better for you to lose one of the parts of your body, than for your whole body to be thrown into hell. **30** If your right hand makes you stumble, cut it off and throw it from you; for it is better for you to lose one of the parts of your body, than for your whole body to go into hell.

31 'It was said, 'Whoever sends his wife away, let him give her a certificate of divorce'; **32** but I say to you that everyone who divorces his wife, except for the reason of unchastity, makes her commit adultery; and whoever marries a divorced woman commits adultery.

33 'Again, you have heard that the ancients were told, 'You shall not make false vows, but shall fulfill your vows to the Lord.' **34** But I say to you, make no oath at all, either by heaven, for it is the throne of God, **35** or by the earth, for it is the footstool of His feet, or by Jerusalem, for it is the city of the great King. **36** Nor shall you make an oath by your head, for you cannot make one hair white or black. **37** But let your statement be, 'Yes, yes' or 'No, no'; anything beyond these is of evil.

38 'You have heard that it was said, 'An eye for an eye, and a tooth for a tooth.' **39** But I say to you, do not resist an evil person; but whoever slaps you on your right cheek, turn the other to him also. **40** If anyone wants to sue you and take your shirt, let him have your coat also. **41** Whoever forces you to go one mile, go with him two. **42** Give to him who asks of you, and do not turn away from him who wants to borrow from you.

43 'You have heard that it was said, 'You shall love your neighbor and hate your enemy.' **44** But I say to you, love your enemies and pray for those who persecute you, **45** so that you may be sons of your Father who is in heaven; for He causes His sun to rise on the evil and the good, and sends rain on the righteous and the unrighteous. **46** For if you love those who love you, what reward do you have? Do not even the tax collectors do the same? **47** If you greet only your brothers, what more are you doing than others? Do not even the Gentiles do the same? **48** Therefore you are to be perfect, as your heavenly Father is perfect."

1. Verse 21 says, "You have heard . . ." Where would the Jews have heard those words? Who are "the ancients" Jesus references?

2. The word "But" usually indicates a contrast. What contrast is Jesus making between what the people have heard from the ancients and what He is saying to them?

3. What are some specific relational issues that Jesus identifies in this section?

4. Underline and summarize the "but I say to you" sections of Jesus' instructions.

5. What is the responsibility of a follower of Christ seen in verses 23–26? Why would verse 25 use the word "quickly?" How does Romans 12:18 help in understanding a believer's role in conflict with another?

Application

In this passage, Jesus is teaching that thoughts are just as important as deeds, emotions just as important as actions. How does this help us define and confess our sin?

A DEEPER LOOK

Verse 48 is perhaps the most difficult verse to understand in this section of Scripture. But this is not the first time God has commanded it. Read Leviticus 11:44, Genesis 17:1, and Deuteronomy 18:13.

Who is perfect?

What does He promise? See Jeremiah 24:7, Philippians 2:12–13, 1 Thessalonians 5:23–24, Philippians 3:12–16

Is it possible to fulfill Christ's command to be perfect? If so, how? What helpful instruction do we read in Hebrews 12:1–3?

STUDY THREE
Giving, Praying, Fasting, and Treasure

Hypocrisy is the enemy of every child of God who desires to live in a way that pleases the Father, so Jesus began this passage with a warning. The practices covered in this section of Jesus' sermon are often referred to as spiritual disciplines, but when pursued with "who's watching?" in mind, the blessing vanishes. As believers in Jesus, whether we are giving, fasting, praying, or serving, we do all in the name and for the glory of God (Colossians 3:17, 1 Corinthians 10:31). That puts our entire lives in spiritual perspective. Christians cannot compartmentalize. Everything we do is an act of worship, an opportunity to bless the Lord and the people around us. Why? Very simply, so that we will grow in the likeness of Christ. That's the big picture Jesus was trying to paint for all who had eyes to see. Pride, greed, rage, and revenge no longer satisfy when we seek to live pleasing only the Lord.

Matthew 6:1–15

"'Beware of practicing your righteousness before men to be noticed by them; otherwise you have no reward with your Father who is in heaven.

2 'So when you give to the poor, do not sound a trumpet before you, as the hypocrites do in the synagogues and in the streets, so that they may be honored by men. Truly I say to you, they have their reward in full. **3** But when you give to the poor, do not let your left hand know what your right hand is doing, **4** so that your giving will be in secret; and your Father who sees what is done in secret will reward you.

5 'When you pray, you are not to be like the hypocrites; for they love to stand and pray in the synagogues and on the street corners so that they may be seen by men. Truly I say to you, they have their reward in full. **6** But you, when you pray, go into your inner room, close your door and pray to your Father who is in secret, and your Father who sees what is done in secret will reward you.

7 'And when you are praying, do not use meaningless repetition as the Gentiles do, for they suppose that they will be heard for their many words. 8 So do not be like them; for your Father knows what you need before you ask Him.

9 'Pray, then, in this way:
'Our Father who is in heaven,
Hallowed be Your name.
10 'Your kingdom come.
Your will be done,
On earth as it is in heaven.
11 'Give us this day our daily bread.
12 'And forgive us our debts, as we also have forgiven our debtors.
13 'And do not lead us into temptation, but deliver us from evil. [For Yours is the kingdom and the power and the glory forever. Amen.']
14 For if you forgive others for their transgressions, your heavenly Father will also forgive you. 15 But if you do not forgive others, then your Father will not forgive your transgressions."

1. In this passage, Jesus again uses comparisons and contrasts. What is the overall warning in verse 1?

2. Summarize what Jesus teaches us to do and not do in verses 2–4.

3. They may sound strange to modern ears, but Jesus is referencing (and condemning) common religious practices of the day in verses 2–8. What does "sounding a trumpet" or "praying on a street corner" look like in our self-promoting culture today?

4. What does Jesus say about praying hypocrites in verse 5?

5. We know Jesus wasn't prohibiting public prayer in verse 6 (see Acts 12:12, 1 Timothy 2:8). What is the "spirit" behind His instruction/exhortation there?

6. Verses 2–7 are about both giving and praying. What does Jesus reiterate about the Father and His character (v. 4, 6)? Why is that encouragement essential to these practices?

7. Jesus models how to pray for believers in verses 9–13. What areas of life does He, through His prayer, teach us to bring to our Father?

Application

While Jesus' prayer in verses 9–13 isn't the only way to pray, we should pay attention how the Son of God approaches His Father. He was praying, but He was also teaching. Reflect on the needs or themes that are a part of your prayer life. Is your heart inclined toward the kinds of things Jesus brings to the throne of grace (Hebrews 4:16)? How does 1 John 5:14–15 instruct and encourage you?

A DEEPER LOOK

What happens in your life and heart when you harbor unforgiveness? How does unforgiveness affect your relationship with God?

Use these passages to answer:

Psalms 103:12   Jeremiah 31:34

Proverbs 28:13   Micah 7:18–19

Isaiah 43:25

Matthew 6:16–24
"16 'Whenever you fast, do not put on a gloomy face as the hypocrites do, for they neglect their appearance so that they will be noticed by men when they are fasting. Truly I say to you, they have their reward in full. 17 But you, when

you fast, anoint your head and wash your face **18** so that your fasting will not be noticed by men, but by your Father who is in secret; and your Father who sees what is done in secret will reward you.

19 'Do not store up for yourselves treasures on earth, where moth and rust destroy, and where thieves break in and steal. **20** But store up for yourselves treasures in heaven, where neither moth nor rust destroys, and where thieves do not break in or steal; **21** for where your treasure is, there your heart will be also.

22 'The eye is the lamp of the body; so then if your eye is clear, your whole body will be full of light. **23** But if your eye is bad, your whole body will be full of darkness. If then the light that is in you is darkness, how great is the darkness!

24 'No one can serve two masters; for either he will hate the one and love the other, or he will be devoted to one and despise the other. You cannot serve God and wealth."

1. Summarize what Jesus is teaching about in this passage.

2. Circle the word "but" in these passages. What contrasts are Jesus making?

3. Read these passages and list the reasons for fasting demonstrated there: 2 Samuel 1:12, Ezra 8:21–23, Daniel 9:2–5, and Acts 13:1–3.

4. What does it mean in verse 20 in Matthew to "store up treasure in heaven" (Colossians 3:1–3)? How is this unseen treasure better than what is right in front of us?

5. How is the eye the "lamp of the body?" How do our eyes influence what and where our treasures are?

6. What does it mean to "serve two masters" (v. 24)?

Application

What do you treasure? How do we serve our possessions? How are you storing up treasures in heaven?

A DEEPER LOOK

Sometimes it is hard to imagine the glory of storing up treasures in heaven when there is so much our eyes can see that our hearts desire. The promise of immediate gratification tempts us to accumulate. Read and meditate on these verses about God's future rewards for His children. How do they encourage you? How do they convict you?

Luke 6:38

Colossians 3:23–24

1 Corinthians 2:9

1 Timothy 6:17–19

1 Corinthians 15:58

Hebrews 6:10–12

STUDY FOUR
Anxiety and Judgment

Jesus was able to teach in a way that both comforted and admonished. Jesus knew His audience and addressed their unseen — maybe even unspoken — fears. And His examples were right before their eyes, ever-present reminders that God is in control. As birds soared overhead and the scent of lilies drifted on the breeze, Jesus pointed to His Father's power and faithfulness. Certainly we are to be concerned with the practical things of life, but Jesus said worrying about them is sin, distracting us from the One who supplies every need. And while we can hold each other accountable, our preoccupation with our neighbor's sin must not keep us from examining our own hearts. If you want fairness, He said, use the same standard on your life that you apply to your brother. Clear sight comes from a clean heart. Seek that first.

Matthew 6:25–34

"**25** 'For this reason I say to you, do not be worried about your life, as to what you will eat or what you will drink; nor for your body, as to what you will put on. Is not life more than food, and the body more than clothing? **26** Look at the birds of the air, that they do not sow, nor reap nor gather into barns, and yet your heavenly Father feeds them. Are you not worth much more than they? **27** And who of you by being worried can add a single hour to his life? **28** And why are you worried about clothing? Observe how the lilies of the field grow; they do not toil nor do they spin, **29** yet I say to you that not even Solomon in all his glory clothed himself like one of these. **30** But if God so clothes the grass of the field, which is alive today and tomorrow is thrown into the furnace, will He not much more clothe you? You of little faith! **31** Do not worry then, saying, 'What will we eat?' or 'What will we drink?' or 'What will we wear for clothing?' **32** For the Gentiles eagerly seek all these things; for your heavenly Father knows that you need all these things. **33** But seek first His kingdom and His righteousness, and all these things will be added to you.

34 'So do not worry about tomorrow; for tomorrow will care for itself. Each day has enough trouble of its own."

1. Write down the questions Jesus asks in this passage.

2. What examples does Jesus use to illustrate His point? Why do you think He used those images? What lessons to do these examples teach?

3. What does verse 33 mean? What assurance does Jesus provide?

4. Jesus begins and ends this section of his teaching with the same exhortation. What is it? Why is this a futile activity?

Application

What do you worry about most? How does worrying affect your life? What keeps you from trusting God with these things? (1 Chronicles 16:11)

A DEEPER LOOK

What is the difference between worrying about the future and planning for the future? How can you plan and prepare without worrying? Read the verses below for guidance.

Psalms 84:11–12

Proverbs 16:9

Psalms 90:12

Proverbs 21:5

Proverbs 3:5–6

James 1:5

Proverbs 14:8

Matthew 7:1–6

"'Do not judge so that you will not be judged. **2** For in the way you judge, you will be judged; and by your standard of measure, it will be measured to you. **3** Why do you look at the speck that is in your brother's eye, but do not notice the log that is in your own eye? **4** Or how can you say to your brother, 'Let me take the speck out of your eye,' and behold, the log is in your own eye? **5** You hypocrite, first take the log out of your own eye, and then you will see clearly to take the speck out of your brother's eye.

6 'Do not give what is holy to dogs, and do not throw your pearls before swine, or they will trample them under their feet, and turn and tear you to pieces.'"

1. What warnings does Jesus give about judging?

2. What is the contrast and indictment in verse 3?

3. What sin does Jesus accuse His hearers of in verse 5? What does He say this looks like in relationship in verse 4?

4. How does Jesus describe people who reject the things of God in verse 6?

5. What is the "holy" that Jesus is warning us to protect in verse 6? Said another way, what is dangerous about sharing precious things with those who reject them?

Application

We are called to discern right and wrong, but we are not the one who determines right and wrong. We can find clear "job descriptions" in God's Word. Read 1 Thessalonians 5:19–24 for a picture of what we're called to do as believers. Compare that with the picture we read about in Revelation 6:14–17 of the Day of Judgment when the wrath of the Lamb is on full display. What perspective does this provide?

STUDY FIVE
The Golden Rule, Narrow Gate, Fruit, and Foundation

Jesus concluded His teaching by framing the character of His Father for the children of Israel. Your Creator—Yahweh, the Lord of heaven and earth—is generous. He listens, He responds, He moves. And when you ask for good things, He gives abundantly more. He is so good, in fact, that He takes all the laws man has crafted and sums them up in one statement, bold and broad enough to please Him in every way: treat others the way you want to be treated. Following this command is essential, and Jesus illustrates what falling short looks like using gates, trees, fruit, and houses. Being a disciple of Jesus and following His teaching is not easy, just like entering a narrow gate. False teachers promote a more expedient and self-serving route; be on your guard and examine the fruit of their teaching. Obeying the words of Jesus makes you wise and firm in your faith, in spite of troubles and trials. This is the life of a faithful follower—not absent of pain, but secure in the midst of it, waiting expectantly for His kingdom to come.

Matthew 7:7–14

"7 'Ask, and it will be given to you; seek, and you will find; knock, and it will be opened to you. 8 For everyone who asks receives, and he who seeks finds, and to him who knocks it will be opened. 9 Or what man is there among you who, when his son asks for a loaf, will give him a stone? 10 Or if he asks for a fish, he will not give him a snake, will he? **11** If you then, being evil, know how to give good gifts to your children, how much more will your Father who is in heaven give what is good to those who ask Him!

12 'In everything, therefore, treat people the same way you want them to treat you, for this is the Law and the Prophets.

13 'Enter through the narrow gate; for the gate is wide and the way is broad that leads to destruction, and there are many who enter through it. **14** For the gate is small and the way is narrow that leads to life, and there are few who find it."

1. What is the progression of instructions in verse 7?

2. How does verse 11 clarify what (and from whom) we should be seeking?

3. What real-life example does Jesus use to explain the character of God in verses 9–11?

4. The word "therefore" always points the reader back to a previous statement of truth as the basis of a new instruction or idea. (What is the "therefore" *there for*?) What is the basis or reason for the Golden Rule presented in verse 12?

5. Compare and contrast the two paths that Jesus presents in verses 13 and 14.

6. In your own words, describe what Jesus is saying about the gate to life.

Application

Do you picture your Heavenly Father as a Giver of good gifts or as a Deity who denies and rejects? How does this passage challenge that? How does the life of Jesus on earth—as Emmanuel—help give a fresh perspective?

Matthew 7:15–23

"**15** 'Beware of the false prophets, who come to you in sheep's clothing, but inwardly are ravenous wolves. **16** You will know them by their fruits. Grapes are not gathered from thorn bushes nor figs from thistles, are they? **17** So every good tree bears good fruit, but the bad tree bears bad fruit. **18** A good tree cannot produce bad fruit, nor can a bad tree produce good fruit. **19** Every tree that does not bear good fruit is cut down and thrown into the fire. **20** So then, you will know them by their fruits.

21 'Not everyone who says to Me, 'Lord, Lord,' will enter the kingdom of heaven, but he who does the will of My Father who is in heaven will enter. **22** Many will say to Me on that day, 'Lord, Lord, did we not prophesy in Your name, and in Your name cast out demons, and in Your name perform many miracles?' **23** And then I will declare to them, 'I never knew you; depart from Me, you who practice lawlessness.'"

1. What warning does Jesus give in verse 15? How does Jesus say false teachers can be identified?

2. Jesus uses fruit as a metaphor. What are the examples of good and bad fruits, spiritually speaking? (See Galatians 5:19–23)

3. How does the scene Jesus describes in verses 21–23 relate to verses 15–20?

4. What is the effect of false teaching on the hearers? (See also Luke 6:39)

5. Who is the ultimate authority on "that day" regarding entrance into the kingdom of heaven? (vv. 22–23)

6. According to Jesus' response in verse 23, what matters most to Him?

Application

Has your decision to follow Jesus radically changed your life? Has your decision to follow Jesus been costly to you? In what ways?

A DEEPER LOOK

What is difficult about identifying false teachers? What do the verses below tell us about identifying them and their fruits?

Romans 16:17–18   2 Timothy 3:13

2 Corinthians 11:13–15   2 Timothy 4:3–4

Colossians 2:8   1 John 4:1

What is the Christian's responsibility with regard to false teaching?

Romans 16:17–18   1 Timothy 6:20–21

Colossians 2:8

Titus 3:9

1 Thessalonians 5:21

1 John 4:2–3

Matthew 7:24–29

"24 'Therefore everyone who hears these words of Mine and acts on them, may be compared to a wise man who built his house on the rock. 25 And the rain fell, and the floods came, and the winds blew and slammed against that house; and yet it did not fall, for it had been founded on the rock. 26 Everyone who hears these words of Mine and does not act on them, will be like a foolish man who built his house on the sand. 27 The rain fell, and the floods came, and the winds blew and slammed against that house; and it fell—and great was its fall."

28 When Jesus had finished these words, the crowds were amazed at His teaching; 29 for He was teaching them as one having authority, and not as their scribes."

1. Jesus the Carpenter ends His sermon with an illustration about building houses.

   In what ways does His illustration demonstrate they are alike?

   How are they different?

2. What does it mean to "act on" the words of Jesus?

3. What is the consequence of not acting on the words of Jesus? (v. 27)

4. Look back at Matthew 5:1–2. Who was Jesus originally teaching? Who is seen at the end of His sermon in Matthew 7:28?

5. What does verse 28 tell us about the crowd's response to Jesus' sermon? Read James 1:22–25 and describe what Scripture says is heart-level response for those who hear the Word.

Application

Evaluate the foundation on which you've built your "house" — is it rock or sand? Has it been tested? Does anything need to change before the next storm comes?

WRAPPING UP

From Healer to Leader, Shepherd to Teacher, Jesus is showing Himself to be amazing in every way. The Sermon on the Mount is straightforward, but has great depth and, if understood rightly, can transform how we live.

In general, people seem to find it easier to follow a to-do list or live by a set of commands rather than live in relationship with a Savior and Lord. Who is the best and brightest, the strongest and the fastest? Who can check off their list of good behavior first and with the smallest margin of error? But from the very beginning of His instruction, Jesus explained His standards are quite different.

The inadequate and in anguish, the tame and the teachable, the middle man and the mistreated. Not exactly the A team. But God's kingdom isn't for those who boast in themselves and their ability. It's for those who finally recognize they need Jesus, that they are nothing and have nothing without Him. What a blessed revelation!

Notes

~ Map of Jesus in Capernaum ~

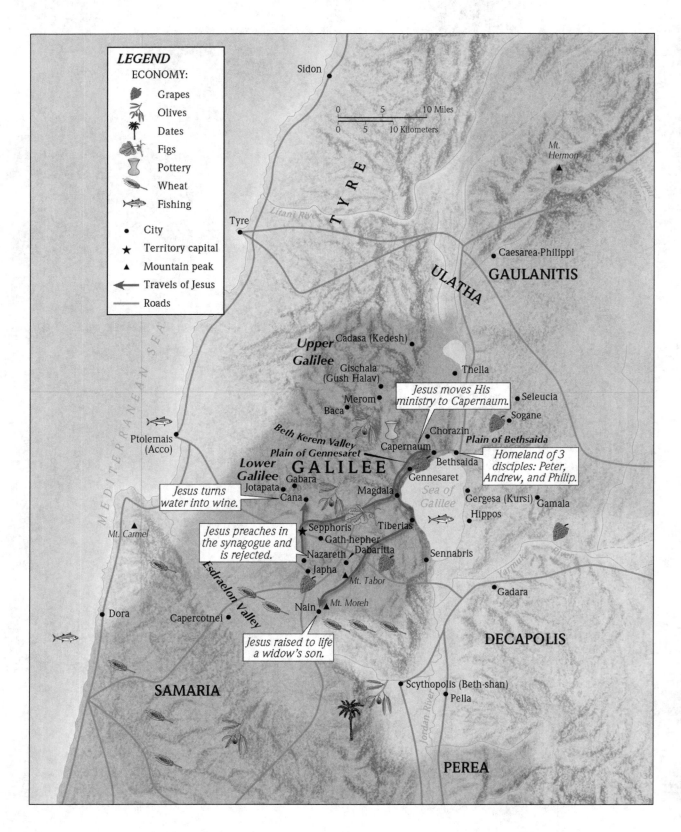

JESUS, THE BURDEN BEARER

"Come to Me, all who are weary and heavy-laden, and I will give you rest. Take My yoke upon you and learn from Me, for I am gentle and humble in heart, and YOU WILL FIND REST FOR YOUR SOULS. For My yoke is easy and My burden is light."
MATTHEW 11:28–30

Think about the burdens of life. Financial burdens—debt, bank account, mortgage, the future. Physical burdens—health, illness, disability, disease. Emotional and mental burdens—conflict, grief, depression, anger. Sometimes it seems not a day goes by that life doesn't hand out some sort of burden to add to the load.

The context in which Jesus presents Himself as the Burden Bearer is unusual. Jesus rebukes His covenant people for their hard hearts and self-sufficiency. The Law had become an obstacle that kept them from simply coming to Him. Layers of religious legislation dictated conduct in relationships, health, work, and worship. The Law was the greatest burden of all.

The Jews were trying to earn God's favor by working as hard as they could to keep all of the rules, many of which they had created themselves. The religious leaders demanded the people come to the Law for salvation. Jesus invited all the weary and broken sinners to come to *Him*.

And here is the glorious hope: when we come to Him, He doesn't leave us as we are. Not only does He promise rest, He provides transformation. This gentle, humble Savior wants to teach us, replacing the heavy burden of self-righteousness with His easy yoke of grace. United with Him for eternity, we have strength to bear whatever comes our way with joy.

STUDY ONE
Jesus Heals a Centurion's Servant

Loss is one of the heaviest burdens to bear. In this passage, loss weighed heavily on people from either end of the social spectrum—a professional soldier and a helpless widow. Death makes no distinctions. It is significant and instructive to see a man of privilege and power care so much about a lowly servant. The centurion's faith played a role in Jesus' healing the slave and, in this moment, the centurion received his greatest commendation of all—praise of the Messiah. A Gentile believed, and he was blessed. Yet there is nothing equal to a mother's grief. She was overwhelmed by sorrow, and Jesus was overcome with compassion. Jesus reached out to touch the open casket, and the dead man's life returned. Jesus restored hope for the widow by lifting the heavy burden that would have caused unbearable sorrow.

Luke 7:1–17

"When He had completed all His discourse in the hearing of the people, He went to Capernaum.

2 And a centurion's slave, who was highly regarded by him, was sick and about to die. **3** When he heard about Jesus, he sent some Jewish elders asking Him to come and save the life of his slave. **4** When they came to Jesus, they earnestly implored Him, saying, 'He is worthy for You to grant this to him; **5** for he loves our nation and it was he who built us our synagogue.' **6** Now Jesus started on His way with them; and when He was not far from the house, the centurion sent friends, saying to Him, 'Lord, do not trouble Yourself further, for I am not worthy for You to come under my roof; **7** for this reason I did not even consider myself worthy to come to You, but just say the word, and my servant will be healed. **8** For I also am a man placed under authority, with soldiers under me; and I say to this one, 'Go!' and he goes, and to another, 'Come!' and he comes, and to my slave, 'Do this!' and he does it.' **9** Now when Jesus heard this, He marveled at him, and turned and said to the crowd that was following Him, 'I say to you, not even in Israel have I found such great faith.' **10** When those who had been sent returned to the house, they found the slave in good health.

11 Soon afterwards He went to a city called Nain; and His disciples were going along with Him, accompanied by a large crowd. **12** Now as He approached the gate of the city, a dead man was being carried out, the only son of his mother, and she was a widow; and a sizeable crowd from the city was with her. **13** When the Lord saw her, He felt compassion for her, and said to her, 'Do not weep.' **14** And He came up and touched the coffin; and the bearers came to a halt. And He said, 'Young man, I say to you, arise!' **15** The dead man sat up and began to speak. And Jesus gave him back to his mother. **16** Fear gripped them all, and they began glorifying God, saying, 'A great prophet has arisen among us!' and, 'God has visited His people!' **17** This report concerning Him went out all over Judea and in all the surrounding district."

1. What "discourse" is Luke referring to in verse 1? (see also Matthew 5–7)

2. Who are the characters in this passage? Underline them.

3. Who "vouched" for the centurion in verse 3? What character traits of the centurion does their endorsement highlight? (vv. 4–5)

4. What is significant about the relationship between the centurion and the Jewish elders?

5. What was the centurion's belief about Jesus (vv. 6–8)?

NOTE: A centurion was a Roman officer in charge of 100 men. The first Gentile convert was Cornelius, a centurion mentioned in Acts 10:1 and 22.

6. What did Jesus say about the centurion? What was significant about this?

7. What did Jesus do for the slave and how did He do it? (v. 10)

8. What's important about this scene in verses 11–17? What is recorded in verse 13 that moved Jesus to compassion in verse 14?

NOTE: "Under the Mosaic dispensation no legal provision was made for the maintenance of widows. They were left dependent partly on the affection of relations, more especially of the eldest son, whose birthright, or extra share of the property, imposed such a duty upon him..." (from *Smith's Bible Dictionary*, www.biblestudytools.com)

9. What did Jesus say and do in this scene? What is significant about verse 14? See Numbers 19:11–13 and Leviticus 21:11.

NOTE: This is the first account in Scripture of Jesus raising someone from the dead.

10. What attributes of God do you see expressed through His Son?

11. What is the response of the crowd? (Note the progression in verse 16.) What did they say? What did they not say?

12. Why would Luke include these two stories? How are they alike? How are they different?

Application
The centurion understood authority. List the people or institutions that have authority over you. Your tenderness toward authority often corresponds to the measure of humility you possess. How do you respond to authority? (Romans 13:1–2)

A DEEPER LOOK
Luke's account tells of a Gentile centurion who was blessed for his relationship with the Jewish community where he lived and served. This was notable because, at this time in history, Jews and Gentiles typically tolerated each other at best. This man went above and beyond to demonstrate his respect and affection for the Jewish people.

Read the verses below and note what God says about His people, the Jews. How does the Lord feel about His people? How are we to treat and respond to them?

Genesis 12:1–3   Psalms 122:6–9   Romans 1:16

Deuteronomy 14:2   Isaiah 62:1–7   Romans 10:1, 12–13

2 Samuel 7:23–24   Zechariah 2:8   Romans 15:27

STUDY TWO
A Deputation from John

Everyone wrestles with the burden of doubt, and here we see that even John the Baptist needed to make sure Jesus was who He said He was. John was faithful and steadfast in his calling, but still just a man. But what an example he set for us! Instead of murmuring to himself or stirring up strife among his followers, John went straight to the Source. He needed assurance, and Jesus reminded John that He had given it many times over, in healing, cleansing, and blessing. Then, Jesus gives more grace: He publicly honors His forerunner by speaking "well done" over his life in the hearing of a diverse crowd. The tax collectors and ordinary folks who experienced forgiveness heard Jesus' words and agreed. But neither John nor Jesus would fit in the box the Pharisees and lawyers built to hold their righteous expectations. Their "wisdom" was offensive to Jesus, and their rejection was costly.

Luke 7:18–35

"18 The disciples of John reported to him about all these things. 19 Summoning two of his disciples, John sent them to the Lord, saying, 'Are You the Expected One, or do we look for someone else?' 20 When the men came to Him, they said, 'John the Baptist has sent us to You, to ask, 'Are You the Expected One, or do we look for someone else?' 21 At that very time He cured many people of diseases and afflictions and evil spirits; and He gave sight to many who were blind. 22 And He answered and said to them, 'Go and report to John what you have seen and heard: the blind receive sight, the lame walk, the lepers are cleansed, and the deaf hear, the dead are raised up, the poor have the gospel preached to them. 23 Blessed is he who does not take offense at Me.'

24 When the messengers of John had left, He began to speak to the crowds about John, 'What did you go out into the wilderness to see? A reed shaken by the wind? 25 But what did you go out to see? A man dressed in soft clothing? Those who are splendidly clothed and live in luxury are found in royal palaces! 26 But what did you go out to see? A prophet? Yes, I say to you, and one who is more than a prophet.

27 This is the one about whom it is written,

'Behold, I send My messenger ahead of You,
Who will prepare Your way before You.'

28 I say to you, among those born of women there is no one greater than John; yet he who is least in the kingdom of God is greater than he.' 29 When all the people and the tax collectors heard this, they acknowledged God's justice, having been baptized with the baptism of John. 30 But the Pharisees and the lawyers rejected God's purpose for themselves, not having been baptized by John.

31 'To what then shall I compare the men of this generation, and what are they like? 32 They are like children who sit in the market place and call to one another, and they say, 'We played the flute for you, and you did not dance; we sang a dirge, and you did not weep.' 33 For John the Baptist has come eating no bread and drinking no wine, and you say, 'He has a demon!' 34 The Son of Man has come eating and drinking, and you say, 'Behold, a gluttonous man and a drunkard, a friend of tax collectors and sinners!' 35 Yet wisdom is vindicated by all her children.'"

1. What did John the Baptist—through his disciples—want to know from Jesus? (see Matthew 11:2) What was going on at the moment the question was posed? (v. 21)

2. How did Jesus answer John's disciples? Then what did Jesus do? (vv. 24–28)

3. How does this authenticate Jesus' identity? (Isaiah 61:1; Isaiah 35:5–6)

4. Why did Jesus defend John's identity at this time? (v. 29)

5. What are the two groups of people described by Jesus (verses 29–30)?

6. Verses 31–35 expound on the second group of people. How does Jesus describe them? What is He saying about their hearts? How did they "miss the point?"

Application

Where do doubts show up in your life? How do you handle unanswered questions? Does it encourage you to see that someone like John the Baptist struggled with doubts about Jesus?

 **STUDY THREE**
Come to Me

Accountability can be a double-edged sword. It is a gift to receive special responsibility or knowledge, but enlightenment can become a burden if not responded to rightly. This is the situation for the cities Jesus condemned in this passage. He blessed them by performing wondrous works there—for their good and His glory—and by providing an opportunity to see, hear, turn, and live. But they were unresponsive. The blind continued in darkness. The deaf chose silence. The dead remained lifeless. Their hardened hearts could have been set free; instead only judgment awaited them. Then we hear a joyful shift in tone as Jesus presented a contrast. Those who accept and respond to His revelation are pleasing to the Father and welcome in His Kingdom. The invitation is to exchange our heavy load for an easy yoke and light burden. All who are weighed down by sin now have a place to rest in Jesus Christ our Burden Bearer.

Matthew 11:20–30

"**20** Then He began to denounce the cities in which most of His miracles were done, because they did not repent. **21** 'Woe to you, Chorazin! Woe to you, Bethsaida! For if the miracles had occurred in Tyre and Sidon which occurred in you, they would have repented long ago in sackcloth and ashes. **22** Nevertheless I say to you, it will be more tolerable for Tyre and Sidon in the day of judgment than for you. **23** And you, Capernaum, will not be exalted to heaven, will you? You will descend to Hades; for if the miracles had occurred in Sodom which occurred in you, it would have remained to this day. **24** Nevertheless I say to you that it will be more tolerable for the land of Sodom in the day of judgment, than for you.'

25 At that time Jesus said, 'I praise You, Father, Lord of heaven and earth, that You have hidden these things from the wise and intelligent and have revealed them to infants. **26** Yes, Father, for this way was well-pleasing in Your sight. **27** All things have been handed over to Me by My Father; and no one knows the Son except the Father; nor does anyone know the Father except the Son, and anyone to whom the Son wills to reveal Him.

28 'Come to Me, all who are weary and heavy-laden, and I will give you rest. **29** Take My yoke upon you and learn from Me, for I am gentle and humble in heart, and you will find rest for your souls. **30** For My yoke is easy and My burden is light.'"

1. Jesus moves from indicting generations of religious leaders to indicting entire cities. Which cities does He mention? What does verse 20 say He did in those cities?

2. What does Jesus indicate in verses 20–21 would have been the right response to His works?

3. What could "these things" be referring to in verse 25? (see v. 20)

4. Who are the "wise and intelligent?" Who are the "infants?" Which kind of person received favor in the Lord's sight?

5. What does Jesus reveal about Himself and His heart in His prayer to His Father?

6. In light of the context of unrepentant generations and cities, what does Jesus' invitation in verses 28–30 mean? Who is invited? What are they invited to do? What is promised?

Application
How does Jesus describe Himself and His yoke in these verses? What are some lessons He has taught you in the past when you've chosen to take on His yoke and learn from Him?

A DEEPER LOOK
Read Psalms 103.

- List all the attributes of God that you see.

- List all the burdens, expressed or implied, that you see.

- Record the ways in which the psalmist describes God carrying these burdens.

What are your burdens? How does this psalm encourage you in knowing Jesus as your Burden Bearer?

STUDY FOUR
Jesus Relates to Women

Nothing moved the heart of Jesus more than a repentant sinner. In this scene, Simon saw a scandal around his dinner table—a woman of immoral reputation touching a powerful and influential Teacher. But all Jesus saw was love. Simon wanted to rub elbows with the "Man of the hour" in Israel. The woman, in humility, came only to wash His feet with her grateful tears. Jesus forced Simon to take a hard look at the woman and at himself and used the story of a man deeply in debt as a mirror. Jesus proclaimed the woman forgiven because of her faith, and pointed out that Simon's failure to love revealed his faith was lacking. It didn't take long for the good news of Jesus to spread. Soon, more women were unburdened from sickness and sin, and responded in worship by ministering to Him.

Luke 7:36–50

"**36** Now one of the Pharisees was requesting Him to dine with him, and He entered the Pharisee's house and reclined at the table. **37** And there was a woman in the city who was a sinner; and when she learned that He was reclining at the table in the Pharisee's house, she brought an alabaster vial of perfume, **38** and standing behind Him at His feet, weeping, she began to wet His feet with her tears, and kept wiping them with the hair of her head, and kissing His feet and anointing them with the perfume. **39** Now when the Pharisee who had invited Him saw this, he said to himself, 'If this man were a prophet He would know who and what sort of person this woman is who is touching Him, that she is a sinner.'

40 And Jesus answered him, 'Simon, I have something to say to you.' And he replied, 'Say it, Teacher.' **41** 'A moneylender had two debtors: one owed five hundred denarii, and the other fifty. **42** When they were unable to repay, he graciously forgave them both. So which of them will love him more?' **43** Simon answered and said, 'I suppose the one whom he forgave more.' And He said to him, 'You have judged correctly.' **44** Turning toward the woman, He said to Simon, 'Do you see this woman? I entered your house; you gave Me no water for My feet, but she has wet My feet with her tears and wiped them with her hair. **45** You gave Me no kiss; but she, since the time I came in, has not ceased to kiss My feet. **46** You did not anoint My head with oil, but she anointed My feet with perfume. **47** For this reason I say to you, her sins, which are many, have been forgiven, for she loved much; but he who is forgiven little, loves little.' **48** Then He said to her, 'Your sins have been forgiven.' **49** Those who were reclining at the table with Him began to say to themselves, 'Who is this man who even forgives sins?' **50** And He said to the woman, 'Your faith has saved you; go in peace.'"

1. Who does Jesus accept a dinner invitation from in verse 36?

2. How is the woman described in verse 37? How is this truthful description of her also gracious?

3. What does this woman do for Jesus?

4. How does Simon, the Pharisee and dinner host, react? What does this say about his heart? How does Jesus' "answer" in verse 40 demonstrate Simon was actually correct about Him in verse 39?

5. What is the message of Jesus' parable to Simon? What is His message to the woman?

6. How does Jesus rebuke Simon and bless the woman at the same time in verses 44–48?

7. What example does Jesus set here about relating to sinners?

8. What does Jesus say saved the woman? (v. 50)

Application

What fills your heart with self-righteousness? What sin—past or present—fills your heart with shame? Are either of these heart conditions a burden that you can allow the Burden Bearer to carry away for you?

Luke 8:1–3
"Soon afterwards, He began going around from one city and village to another, proclaiming and preaching the kingdom of God. The twelve were with Him, ² and also some women who had been healed of evil spirits and sicknesses: Mary who was called Magdalene, from whom seven demons had gone out, ³ and Joanna the wife of Chuza, Herod's steward, and Susanna, and many others who were contributing to their support out of their private means."

1. What does verse 1 say Jesus is doing?

2. What are the demographics of Jesus' followers in these verses?

3. As the wife of Chuza who served in the court of Herod Antipas, Joanna must have been a woman of wealth and status. At one time, Mary Magdalene had been a societal outcast, suffering from demon possession. What does their proximity to Jesus and His ministry say to you?

Application

How can you use your time, talents, and resources to help love others, serve the Lord, and build the kingdom of God?

STUDY FIVE
The Pharisees Rebuked

Just when the light was about to dawn for the people of Israel, the Pharisees cast more shadows. Jesus demonstrated His authority over demons, and the people responded expectantly. But instead of shepherding them toward their Savior, the religious leaders accused Jesus of sorcery. Jesus used simple logic to upend their charges: how would it benefit Satan to cast out a demon from this man? Jesus honored His Father by naming the Spirit of God as the source of His power. He then gave a grave warning to anyone tempted to speak against the Spirit and His ministry. The Pharisees' words against Jesus revealed a poisonous root growing in their hearts, and that evil nature tied them more closely with hell than heaven. Jesus could do a million miracles, and they would still be blinded by their pride and self-righteousness. As a result of these over-the-line accusations, Jesus completely disconnected with the religious Jews, giving highest priority to His relationships with those who loved Him and His Father.

Matthew 12:22–37

"**22** Then a demon-possessed man who was blind and mute was brought to Jesus, and He healed him, so that the mute man spoke and saw. **23** All the crowds were amazed, and were saying, 'This man cannot be the Son of David, can he?' **24** But when the Pharisees heard this, they said, 'This man casts out demons only by Beelzebul the ruler of the demons.'

25 And knowing their thoughts Jesus said to them, 'Any kingdom divided against itself is laid waste; and any city or house divided against itself will not stand. **26** If Satan casts out Satan, he is divided against himself; how then will his kingdom stand? **27** If I by Beelzebul cast out demons, by whom do your sons cast them out? For this reason they will be your judges. **28** But if I cast out demons by the Spirit of God, then the kingdom of God has come upon you. **29** Or how can anyone enter the strong man's house and carry off his property, unless he first binds the strong man? And then he will plunder his house.

30 He who is not with Me is against Me; and he who does not gather with Me scatters. **31** 'Therefore I say to you, any sin and blasphemy shall be forgiven people, but blasphemy against the Spirit shall not be forgiven. **32** Whoever speaks a word against the Son of Man, it shall be forgiven him; but whoever speaks against the Holy Spirit, it shall not be forgiven him, either in this age or in the age to come.

33 'Either make the tree good and its fruit good, or make the tree bad and its fruit bad; for the tree is known by its fruit. **34** You brood of vipers, how can you, being evil, speak what is good? For the mouth speaks out of that which fills the heart. **35** The good man brings out of his good treasure what is good; and the evil man brings out of his evil treasure what is evil. **36** But I tell you that every careless word that people speak, they shall give an accounting for it in the day of judgment. **37** For by your words you will be justified, and by your words you will be condemned.'"

1. What was the question of the crowd after Jesus healed the demon-possessed man? What truth does it appear they are considering? (v. 23)

2. What did the Pharisees call Jesus in verse 24? What was their accusation?

3. How did Jesus validate His authority for casting out demons in this passage?

4. What two kingdoms did Jesus present in verses 25–29?

5. What sin does Jesus speak about in verses 30–32? How is this a warning to the Pharisees?

6. How do Jesus' comments on the evidence of what is in their hearts in verses 33–37 connect to the sin described in verses 30–32?

7. Read Proverbs 29:1, Matthew 10:33, John 3:18–19, John 12:48, and Hebrews 12:25. What is the unpardonable sin that can be committed today?

8. How does Jesus connect the heart and the mouth? (Ephesians 5:3–4, 12; Colossians 3:17; James 1:19; 3:1–12)

Application

What do your words reveal about your heart? Is what emerges during a time of temptation or trial (or even traffic!) anything like what spills out when all is well and life is good? Pray that the Refiner's fire would test and try your speech and burn off anything that is not pleasing or glorifying to Him. (Psalms 139:23–24)

A DEEPER LOOK

Do you take the power of Satan seriously? Do you believe he is the lion that seeks to devour you at every opportunity? Read these passages about the devil and take note of his power on this earth and his hatred of the things and people of God.

Isaiah 14:12–15   1 Thessalonians 2:18

John 8:44   1 Peter 5:8

John 10:10   1 John 3:8

2 Corinthians 4:4   1 John 5:19

Ephesians 6:12   Revelation 12:9–12

Matthew 12:38–50

"**38** Then some of the scribes and Pharisees said to Him, 'Teacher, we want to see a sign from You.' **39** But He answered and said to them, 'An evil and adulterous generation craves for a sign; and yet no sign will be given to it but the sign of Jonah the prophet; **40** for just as Jonah was three days and three nights in the belly of the sea monster, so will the Son of Man be three days and three nights in the heart of the earth. **41** The men of Nineveh will stand up with this generation at the judgment, and will condemn it because they repented at the preaching of Jonah; and behold, something greater than Jonah is here. **42** The Queen of the South will rise up with this generation at the judgment and will condemn it, because she came from the ends of the earth to hear the wisdom of Solomon; and behold, something greater than Solomon is here.

43 'Now when the unclean spirit goes out of a man, it passes through waterless places seeking rest, and does not find it. **44** Then it says, 'I will return to my house from which I came'; and when it comes, it finds it unoccupied, swept, and put in order. **45** Then it goes and takes along with it seven other spirits more wicked than itself, and they go in and live there; and the last state of that man becomes worse than the first. That is the way it will also be with this evil generation.'

46 While He was still speaking to the crowds, behold, His mother and brothers were standing outside, seeking to speak to Him. **47** Someone said to Him, 'Behold, Your mother and Your brothers are standing outside seeking to speak to You.' **48** But Jesus answered the one who was telling Him and said, 'Who is My mother and who are My brothers?' **49** And stretching out His hand toward His disciples, He said, 'Behold My mother and My brothers! **50** For whoever does the will of My Father who is in heaven, he is My brother and sister and mother.'"

1. What were the Pharisees asking for in verse 38? What is ironic about that request?

2. In your own words, explain what Jesus is saying to and about the Pharisees in verses 38–41. What did Jesus say about their desire for a sign (verse 39)? What was their motive for asking?

3. Read and review 1 Kings 10:1–13. What is Jesus saying to the Pharisees using this example (v. 42)?

4. Jesus teaches about demon possession and what happens when a demon is cast out. Look at verse 44. What does it mean that the "house" is "unoccupied?"

5. Read Romans 8:9–11, 1 Corinthians 3:16, 2 Corinthians 13:5, Ephesians 1:13. What must happen to prevent the evil spirit from returning? (v. 45)

6. What relationship did Jesus prioritize in the scene in verses 46–50?

7. What is known from Scripture about how those closest to Jesus felt about Him? See John 7:5 and Mark 3:21–22.

Application
Read Mark 3:21 for more insight into how Jesus' family felt about Him. How important are the opinions of the people closest to you? What can you do to push through the times when you are misunderstood and unsupported?

A DEEPER LOOK

How does it feel to know you are welcome into the family of God through Jesus Christ? Read these verses and write down the benefits of being part of His eternal family.

Romans 8:1–39

2 Peter 1:3–4

Ephesians 1:3–14

1 John 3:1–3

WRAPPING UP

We are deceived when we think we can take care of something on our own, or that we have a concern too small to bring to our Savior. There is no burden that's too heavy for Him to bear. Sin is our greatest burden, and we praise God for sending His Son to carry it away through His blood shed on the cross. Jesus died to remove the unbearable weight of sin, a debt we could never repay, and rose from the dead that we might have new life in Him.

Charles Wesley said it well in his hymn, *And Can It Be?*:

Long my imprisoned spirit lay,
Fast bound in sin and nature's night;
Thine eye diffused a quickening ray—
I woke, the dungeon flamed with light;
My chains fell off, my heart was free,
I rose, went forth, and followed Thee.

Amazing love! How can it be,
That Thou, my God, shouldst die for me?

JESUS, THE STORYTELLER

"All these things Jesus spoke to the crowds in parables, and He did not speak to them without a parable. This was to fulfill what was spoken through the prophet: "I WILL OPEN MY MOUTH IN PARABLES; I WILL UTTER THINGS HIDDEN SINCE THE FOUNDATION OF THE WORLD.""

Matthew 13:34–35

Jesus was a captivating Storyteller. A Pulitzer-prize-winning, *New-York-Times*-bestselling kind of literary genius. And every plot line had a point. From sower and soils to wheat and weeds, Jesus gave the ordinary scenery of every day life a voice. And the stories these characters told promised abundant life and ceaseless hope for those with ears to hear and hearts to believe.

The kingdom of heaven was a common theme Jesus wove through His truth-filled stories. This longed-for kingdom was finally here, He proclaimed, yet the eyes and hearts of the people were closed to the One who ushered it in. But for those who sought understanding, Jesus wanted to be clear: *Receive My words with joy! Let them take root and transform you. I have come to die so that you may live!*

Jesus told simple stories with a profound meaning, and the symbolism was supposed to stick with them. For instance, when a farmer gathered a handful of seeds to toss into his upturned earth, perhaps he would recall the good soil Jesus mentioned and the hundredfold crop that was sown. Perhaps he would remember the hope that stirred inside him as he stood shoulder to shoulder with his neighbors by the sea, mesmerized by the words of the carpenter's Son. Maybe the seed that had been planted in his heart that day would begin to grow.

Jesus called His disciples "blessed," because they were hearing and seeing things Abraham, Moses, and David could only long for. Because of God's Spirit in us, we have that same blessing—hearing, seeing, and understanding the greatest story ever told.

STUDY ONE
Jesus Teaches in Parables

While Jesus' stories are simple, they are not always easy to understand. Sitting in a boat by the sea, Jesus invoked the image of farming to the common folks, who would likely be very familiar with soil, seeds, and the nuances of agriculture. Yet even as Jesus spoke these words, He knew their ears were closed and their hearts were hard. There is blessing to be found, though—the disciples' request for clarity revealed they had a hunger and thirst for deeper things. As a masterful storyteller, Jesus' agrarian scene cuts both ways—judgment to those who refuse to accept Him and life to those who receive His words as truth.

Matthew 13:1–17

"That day Jesus went out of the house and was sitting by the sea. **2** And large crowds gathered to Him, so He got into a boat and sat down, and the whole crowd was standing on the beach.

3 And He spoke many things to them in parables, saying, 'Behold, the sower went out to sow; **4** and as he sowed, some seeds fell beside the road, and the birds came and ate them up. **5** Others fell on the rocky places, where they did not have much soil; and immediately they sprang up, because they had no depth of soil. **6** But when the sun had risen, they were scorched; and because they had no root, they withered away. **7** Others fell among the thorns, and the thorns came up and choked them out. **8** And others fell on the good soil and yielded a crop, some a hundredfold, some sixty, and some thirty. **9** He who has ears, let him hear.'

10 And the disciples came and said to Him, 'Why do You speak to them in parables?' **11** Jesus answered them, 'To you it has been granted to know the mysteries of the kingdom of heaven, but to them it has not been granted. **12** For whoever has, to him more shall be given, and he will have an abundance; but whoever does not have, even what he has shall be taken away from him. **13** Therefore I speak to them in parables; because while seeing they do not see, and while hearing they do not hear, nor do they understand. **14** In their case the prophecy of Isaiah is being fulfilled, which says,

'You will keep on hearing, but will not understand;
You will keep on seeing, but will not perceive;
15 For the heart of this people has become dull,
With their ears they scarcely hear,
And they have closed their eyes,
Otherwise they would see with their eyes,
Hear with their ears,
And understand with their heart and return,
And I would heal them.'

16 But blessed are your eyes, because they see; and your ears, because they hear. **17** For truly I say to you that many prophets and righteous men desired to see what you see, and did not see it, and to hear what you hear, and did not hear it."

1. Describe the scene in verses 1–2 in your own words.

2. Define the word "parable" using a dictionary or www.biblestudytools.com.

3. List the places where the seed was planted. Record what happened to the seed in each place.

4. Why did Jesus teach in this way (verses 11–15)? What is Jesus trying to communicate to the crowd?

5. What are the "mysteries of the kingdom of heaven" in verse 11? (see Colossians 1:26–27)

6. Jesus said He is quoting Isaiah in verses 14–15. Read Isaiah 6. Based on our study so far, how does Isaiah's commission from the Lord compare to Jesus' ministry on earth?

7. What does it mean for a person to "keep on" hearing and seeing but not understand or perceive? (vv. 13–14)

8. How does Jesus diagnose the condition of the people who do not understand His words? (v. 15)

9. Thinking about the Old Testament, who might Jesus have been referring to in verse 17?

Application
Has the Lord ever had to get your attention about a heart issue? How did He do it? How did you respond?

STUDY TWO
The Parable Explained

With the disciples gathered around Him, Jesus explained His parable: four seedtime scenarios and four harvest outcomes with only one that bears fruit. As Jesus dug into the meaning behind the images, we see this isn't a discourse on husbandry; it's an exhortation for eternal life. By design, we have a choice—we can let "the word of the kingdom" be overrun by the brambles and briers of life. Or we can let Jesus provide water and light to cultivate growth for the truth planted in us. Only then can we bear fruit in a dying world.

Matthew 13:18–23

"**18** 'Hear then the parable of the sower. **19** When anyone hears the word of the kingdom and does not understand it, the evil one comes and snatches away what has been sown in his heart. This is the one on whom seed was sown beside the road. **20** The one on whom seed was sown on the rocky places, this is the man who hears the word and immediately receives it with joy; **21** yet he has no firm root in himself, but is only temporary, and when affliction or persecution arises because of the word, immediately he falls away. **22** And the one on whom seed was sown among the thorns, this is the man who hears the word, and the worry of the world and the deceitfulness of wealth choke the word, and it becomes unfruitful. **23** And the one on whom seed was sown on the good soil, this is the man who hears the word and understands it; who indeed bears fruit and brings forth, some a hundredfold, some sixty, and some thirty."

1. Jesus interprets His own parable in verses 18–23.

   • Record the interpretation of each seed's placement and outcome.

   • What is the condition of "the man?"

   • What is the seed?

   • Who could the sower be?

2. Jesus uses the word "hear" four times in this passage. What does Jesus want the hearers to understand in His story?

3. What facilitates an understanding of the Word (v. 23)?

Application

Reflect on your spiritual growth. What would you say, over time, is the fruit of your relationship with Jesus? Give specifics.

STUDY THREE
Tares Among Wheat

This tale is one of sabotage and intrigue. An enemy tried to wreak havoc in the field by sowing damaging weeds into the farmer's healthy crop of wheat. The farmer lets the two plants coexist until harvest time, when a distinction will be made as to what is preserved and what is destroyed. While Jesus provided needed interpretation, one thing is clear: the enemy is always working to corrupt the kingdom's harvest. While on this earth, we are called to love others freely, but we must live distinctly and with discernment. We spend our days alongside those who may appear or even say they are heaven bound, but in reality, their hearts are far from home. The day of judgment will come, and the One who knows our hearts will gather and scatter as His mercy and justice determine. In the meantime, we sow in love and plant with prayer and wait for His return.

Matthew 13:24–30

"**24** Jesus presented another parable to them, saying, 'The kingdom of heaven may be compared to a man who sowed good seed in his field. **25** But while his men were sleeping, his enemy came and sowed tares among the wheat, and went away. **26** But when the wheat sprouted and bore grain, then the tares became evident also. **27** The slaves of the landowner came and said to him, 'Sir, did you not sow good seed in your field? How then does it have tares?' **28** And he said to them, 'An enemy has done this!' The slaves said to him, 'Do you want us, then, to go and gather them up?' **29** But he said, 'No; for while you are gathering up the tares, you may uproot the wheat with them. **30** Allow both to grow together until the harvest; and in the time of the harvest I will say to the reapers, "First gather up the tares and bind them in bundles to burn them up; but gather the wheat into my barn.'"

1. What is Jesus comparing in verse 24?

2. What happened next and why did it happen (verse 25)?

A tare is a species of rye grass that resembles wheat as it begins to grow. But it "behaves" like a weed and is harmful to the plants among which it grows.

3. Why didn't the landowner immediately resolve the issue in the field? (look ahead to v. 38 for clarity about the "field.")

4. In terms of the kingdom of heaven, what is "the harvest" (v. 30)?

5. Spiritually speaking, who are the "tares?" Who is the "wheat?" What does the relationship between the wheat and tares represent?

6. What is the final end for the tares at the time of the harvest?

7. What does the Storyteller want us to understand from this parable?

Application
What are some examples of "weeds" that choke out the Word in your life?

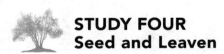

STUDY FOUR
Seed and Leaven

God has always chosen to do big miracles with small things. From the tiny insects that plagued the mighty Egyptians to five smooth stones that slew a giant, size does not matter in the eyes of eternity. While the wheat and tares parable is explained to the disciples, the crowd is given a glimpse into the future of the kingdom of God. It was probably difficult for the Jews to imagine life beyond their "here and now." Jesus was misunderstood on every front, so His proposal must have seemed impossible: how could something like a tiny seed or a batch of yeast change the world? What a gift we have to see in Scripture the humble beginnings of the kingdom of heaven on earth and, today, experience the blessing of its growth.

Matthew 13:31–43

"**31** He presented another parable to them, saying, 'The kingdom of heaven is like a mustard seed, which a man took and sowed in his field; **32** and this is smaller than all other seeds, but when it is full grown, it is larger than the garden plants and becomes a tree, so that the birds of the air come and nest in its branches.'

33 He spoke another parable to them, 'The kingdom of heaven is like leaven, which a woman took and hid in three pecks of flour until it was all leavened.'
34 All these things Jesus spoke to the crowds in parables, and He did not speak to them without a parable.
35 This was to fulfill what was spoken through the prophet:
"I will open My mouth in parables;
I will utter things hidden since the foundation of the world."

36 Then He left the crowds and went into the house. And His disciples came to Him and said, 'Explain to us the parable of the tares of the field.' **37** And He said, 'The one who sows the good seed is the Son of Man, **38** and the field is the world; and as for the good seed, these are the sons of the kingdom; and the tares are the sons of the evil one; **39** and the enemy who sowed them is the devil, and the harvest is the end of the age; and the reapers are angels. **40** So just as the tares are gathered up and burned with fire, so shall it be at the end of the age. **41** The Son of Man will send forth His angels, and they will gather out of His kingdom all stumbling blocks, and those who commit lawlessness, **42** and will throw them into the furnace of fire; in that place there will be weeping and gnashing of teeth. **43** Then the righteous will shine forth as the sun in the kingdom of their Father. He who has ears, let him hear."

1. What is Jesus saying in verses 31–33 about the size and growth of the kingdom of heaven?

2. Use a dictionary to look up the word *leaven*. Write the definitions below.

3. Based on verses 34–35, what was significant about what Jesus was doing in this passage? How does it support His deity?

4. Note and record the change in Jesus' location and audience in verse 36.

5. Again Jesus interprets His words for us in verses 37–43. List the "characters" from the story and what He explains they represent. (vv. 37–39)

6. Circle the word "will" in verses 41–43. What does that verb indicate? What is Jesus saying will happen at the end of the age?

7. What is promised in this passage? What are the warnings?

Application

A mustard seed is about the size of the period at the end of this sentence. Think of other stories in Scripture where God uses something very small to do something great. How does that encourage you?

A DEEPER LOOK

Read Psalms 78:1–7. As followers of Jesus, what is our responsibility as "storytellers?"

Write down the story of God's faithfulness and your growth in Christ.

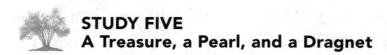

STUDY FIVE
A Treasure, a Pearl, and a Dragnet

Jesus now peppers His disciples with a variety of images, working to get His point across. The rustic, rural sketches are gone; here, we see gleaming treasure, sparkling jewels, and life from the sea. The math is interesting in these stories: the main character gives all he has to gain one thing. What could be so valuable, so extraordinary, that the cost means nothing and the object is everything? It is a joy to see the disciples comprehend the words of Jesus when so often, they seemed to miss His message. Now, with understanding comes accountability. They have been "trained" in the fulfillment and revelation of Jesus and will soon be sent out to spread the Word.

Matthew 13:44–52

"⁴⁴ 'The kingdom of heaven is like a treasure hidden in the field, which a man found and hid again; and from joy over it he goes and sells all that he has and buys that field.

⁴⁵ 'Again, the kingdom of heaven is like a merchant seeking fine pearls, ⁴⁶ and upon finding one pearl of great value, he went and sold all that he had and bought it.

⁴⁷ "Again, the kingdom of heaven is like a dragnet cast into the sea, and gathering fish of every kind; ⁴⁸ and when it was filled, they drew it up on the beach; and they sat down and gathered the good fish into containers, but the bad they threw away. ⁴⁹ So it will be at the end of the age; the angels will come forth and take out the wicked from among the righteous, ⁵⁰ and will throw them into the furnace of fire; in that place there will be weeping and gnashing of teeth.

⁵¹ 'Have you understood all these things?' They said to Him, 'Yes.' ⁵² And Jesus said to them, 'Therefore every scribe who has become a disciple of the kingdom of heaven is like a head of a household, who brings out of his treasure things new and old.'"

1. Record the activity of the man and the merchant in verses 44–45.

2. How does the kingdom of heaven operate in verse 47?

3. How is the parable in verses 47–50 similar to the parable in verses 24–30? How is it different?

4. Based on Luke 5:10, who might Jesus have had in mind in verse 47?

5. What did Jesus want to know in verse 51? Why do you think that was important? (see 2 Timothy 2:7)

How did the disciples respond to Jesus' question? (see Ephesians 1:15–17, 2 Peter 3:18)

6. In verse 52, the word "Therefore" refers back to Jesus' question of the disciples in verse 51. What is Jesus saying about the understanding and responsibility of the disciples?

What is the new and old "treasure" being revealed and fulfilled?

7. What do you learn about God in this passage? What do you learn about His kingdom?

8. What is the emotion named in this section? What does that tell you about the kingdom of heaven?

NOTE: Scholars vary in their interpretation of this parable. Some believe the parables of the treasure and pearl refer to the great value of the kingdom that moves man to do everything he can to possess it. Another interpretation sees the man as Christ (as in verse 37) who sacrifices His life to purchase His people.

Application

Review and reflect on each one of the illustrations Jesus gave in describing the kingdom of heaven. How do Jesus' stories help us understand His heart and His purposes?

A DEEPER LOOK

To deepen your understanding, take some time to dig a little more into this passage about the kingdom of heaven:

- What is the object of each search?

- Who is the man in Matthew 13:44–46? See Hebrews 12:1–2, John 3:16, and 1 Corinthians 6:19–20.

- What is the response of the man to what he finds?

- How does Philippians 3:7–8 help you interpret this passage?

WRAPPING UP

The image of planting and growth has been a frequent picture Jesus used in His parables this week. That language is still common today for those who follow Jesus. We use the allegory because it is descriptive of what we hope and want for our life in Christ: constant growth, perpetual fruit.

We all have a story—a past, a present, and a future. And God has been weaving it together since before we took our first breath on earth. What a gift when our eyes are opened to see it is really His story on display! Thank God that He uses and redeems our past, is transforming us every moment of our present, and has a perfect and prosperous plan for our future!

~ Map of Jesus in Capernaum ~

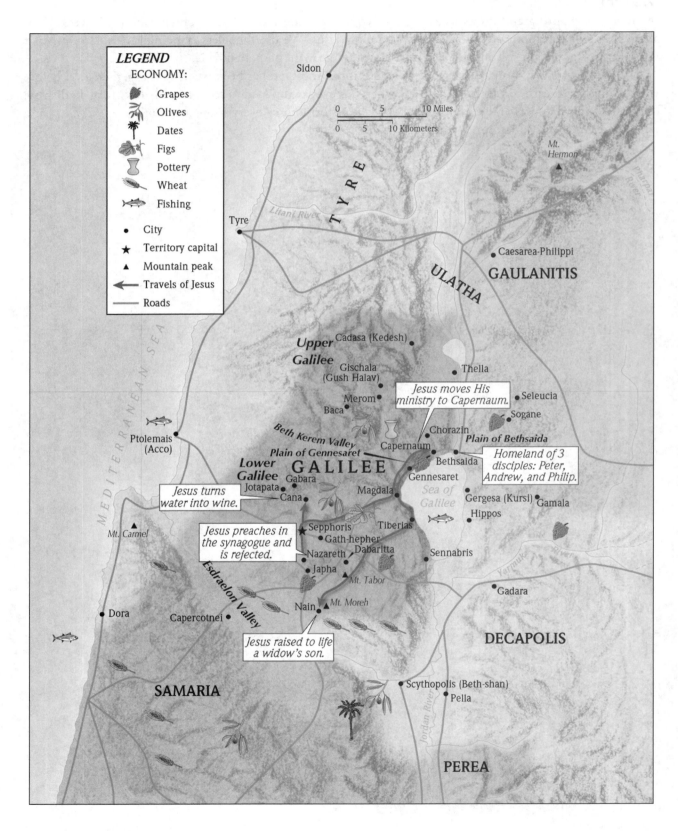

JESUS, THE LIFE GIVER

"And he who does not take his cross and follow after Me is not worthy of Me. He who has found his life will lose it, and he who has lost his life for My sake will find it."
MATTHEW 10:38–39

Whether it was the outskirts of a Gentile village or the heart of His hometown, Jesus encountered need everywhere He went. This week, we see lives brought back from the brink of death—spiritually, emotionally, and physically. The people Jesus met were desperate. And when desperation and compassion intersect, hope is born.

A man tortured by the forces of hell became a new creation through Jesus' merciful rebuke. A woman, alone in her suffering and pain, timidly touched His cloak in faith and was restored to perfect health. A loving father loses his child too soon; Jesus took her hand and brought her back to life.

Over and over, Jesus gladly gave life to all who were "dwelling among the tombs," but ultimately, the greatest gift of life He gave was His own. We were possessed by darkness, sick in our souls and dead in our sins. Jesus meets us at every place of need as our marvelous Light, consoling Cure, and eternal Life.

As Jesus' followers observed these miracles, they grew in their commitment to His "cause." But Jesus' definition of discipleship seemed strange even to His closest friends: loss means gain, He told them, so let go of anything else that has captured your affections, and find all you have been looking for in Me. This message would bring peace to some and feel like the edge of a sword to others. The disciples were learning the life Jesus offered would not be easy, but something inside them whispered it would be worth it.

STUDY ONE
The Sea and the Demoniac

After a full day of ministry, Jesus the Man was weary. Jesus slept so soundly in the back of a boat, He was unaware of the fierce winds and rising waters on the Sea of Galilee. As the disciples' little vessel filled with fear, Jesus stood up and stilled the chaos like a Father quieting an unruly child. And the Twelve were shaken by the power of the Teacher they thought they knew. The stranger they met on the shore knew Jesus all too well: a demon-possessed man, plagued for so long and by so much evil, he and those who knew him had given up hope. Legion acknowledged the Messiah then begged Jesus to send them into a herd of swine. The man, delivered and set right again, knew he had been given back his life. And now he's begging, too—to follow Jesus wherever He went. But Jesus had another plan in mind. He turned this former madman into a missionary. Jesus left behind a life transformed, and there were many more to come.

Mark 4:35–5:20

"**35** On that day, when evening came, He said to them, 'Let us go over to the other side.' **36** Leaving the crowd, they took Him along with them in the boat, just as He was; and other boats were with Him. **37** And there arose a fierce gale of wind, and the waves were breaking over the boat so much that the boat was already filling up. **38** Jesus Himself was in the stern, asleep on the cushion; and they woke Him and said to Him, 'Teacher, do You not care that we are perishing?' **39** And He got up and rebuked the wind and said to the sea, 'Hush, be still.' And the wind died down and it became perfectly calm. **40** And He said to them, 'Why are you afraid? Do you still have no faith?' **41** They became very much afraid and said to one another, 'Who then is this, that even the wind and the sea obey Him?'

1 They came to the other side of the sea, into the country of the Gerasenes. **2** When He got out of the boat, immediately a man from the tombs with an unclean spirit met Him, **3** and he had his dwelling among the tombs. And no one was able to bind him anymore, even with a chain; **4** because he had often been bound with shackles and chains, and the chains had been torn apart by him and the shackles broken in pieces, and no one was strong enough to subdue him. **5** Constantly, night and day, he was screaming among the tombs and in the mountains, and gashing himself with stones. **6** Seeing Jesus from a distance, he ran up and bowed down before Him; **7** and shouting with a loud voice, he said, 'What business do we have with each other, Jesus, Son of the Most High God? I implore You by God, do not torment me!' **8** For He had been saying to him, 'Come out of the man, you unclean spirit!' **9** And He was asking him, 'What is your name?' And he said to Him, 'My name is Legion; for we are many.' **10** And he began to implore Him earnestly not to send them out of the country. **11** Now there was a large herd of swine feeding nearby on the mountain. **12** The demons implored Him, saying, 'Send us into the swine so that we may enter them.' **13** Jesus gave them permission. And coming out, the unclean spirits entered the swine; and the herd rushed down the steep bank into the sea, about two thousand of them; and they were drowned in the sea.

14 Their herdsmen ran away and reported it in the city and in the country. And the people came to see what it was that had happened. **15** They came to Jesus and observed the man who had been demon-possessed sitting down, clothed and in his right mind, the very man who had had the "legion"; and they became frightened. **16** Those who had seen it described to them how it had happened to the demon-possessed man, and all about the swine. **17** And they began to implore Him to leave their region. **18** As He was getting into the boat, the man who had been demon-possessed was imploring Him that he might accompany Him. **19** And He did not let him, but He said to him, 'Go home to your people and report to them what great things the Lord has done for you, and how He had mercy on you.' **20** And he went away and began to proclaim in Decapolis what great things Jesus had done for him; and everyone was amazed."

1. What time of day was it in verse 35? What does verse 36 indicate Jesus had been doing all day?

2. What happens in verse 37? What was Jesus doing in verse 38? What does this say about His humanity?

3. What did the disciples call Him? What does that reveal about their view of Jesus?

4. What did Jesus say and do? Based on the disciples' response in verse 41, do you think Jesus behaved the way they expected Him to?

5. What is different about the disciples' fear in verse 38 and their fear in verse 41?

6. What question did the disciples ask each other in verse 41? What is the answer to this question?

7. Where was the country of the Gerasenes? (use an online resource for your research like www.bible-studytools.com)

8. Who met Jesus as He got out of the boat? Write down the details Mark records for us about this man (his appearance and actions).

9. What is significant about verse 7 (see James 2:19)? What did the demon-possessed man call himself in verse 9 and why?

10. Read verses 9–13. Describe the exchange between the demons and Jesus. What do you observe about the power of Jesus compared to the power of "Legion?"

11. What happened to the unclean spirits upon leaving the man?

12. Describe the condition of the man after the unclean spirits left him. How does this reveal Jesus as Life Giver?

13. How did the people of this area hear about this event? How did they respond? Why do you think they responded that way?

14. What did the restored man want to do (v. 18)? What was Jesus' answer and instruction in verse 19?

15. What did the man do in verse 20? [*For a glimpse ahead at the outcome of his obedience, read Mark 7:31–8:10. This is Jesus' return visit to the Decapolis, after "commissioning" the former demoniac.*]

16. Why was it better for this man to *go and tell about* Jesus than to go *with* Jesus?

Application
Read 2 Corinthians 5:17–18 and record how the truths of this passage are displayed in the encounter in Mark 4. How are they displayed in your life?

"I'm sorry. There's nothing we can do." The woman had probably heard those words more times than she could count over the twelve years she suffered. By now, she resolved this would be her life—constantly weak from loss of blood, shunned by her community, her existence revolving around this uncontrollable, consuming condition. But then, a glimmer of Hope appeared. And she had just enough faith to reach out and touch it. Jesus was busy, headed to the important home of an important man who was in anguish over his little girl. With the crowd so close, maybe no one would notice if she quietly slipped through to grasp at one more chance to be whole. The power that rushed through her was nothing compared to the love that overwhelmed her, as Jesus looked straight into her eyes and spoke life into her heart. He called her "daughter." Now—and forever.

Mark 5:21–43

"**21** When Jesus had crossed over again in the boat to the other side, a large crowd gathered around Him; and so He stayed by the seashore. **22** One of the synagogue officials named Jairus came up, and on seeing Him, fell at His feet **23** and implored Him earnestly, saying, 'My little daughter is at the point of death; please come and lay Your hands on her, so that she will get well and live.' **24** And He went off with him; and a large crowd was following Him and pressing in on Him.

25 A woman who had had a hemorrhage for twelve years, **26** and had endured much at the hands of many physicians, and had spent all that she had and was not helped at all, but rather had grown worse— **27** after hearing about Jesus, she came up in the crowd behind Him and touched His cloak. **28** For she thought, 'If I just touch His garments, I will get well.' **29** Immediately the flow of her blood was dried up; and she felt in her body that she was healed of her affliction. **30** Immediately Jesus, perceiving in Himself that the power proceeding from Him had gone forth, turned around in the crowd and said, 'Who touched My garments?' **31** And His disciples said to Him, 'You see the crowd pressing in on You, and You say, 'Who touched Me?' **32** And He looked around to see the woman who had done this. **33** But the woman fearing and trembling, aware of what had happened to her, came and fell down before Him and told Him the whole truth. **34** And He said to her, 'Daughter, your faith has made you well; go in peace and be healed of your affliction.'

35 While He was still speaking, they came from the house of the synagogue official, saying, 'Your daughter has died; why trouble the Teacher anymore?' **36** But Jesus, overhearing what was being spoken, said to the synagogue official, 'Do not be afraid any longer, only believe.' **37** And He allowed no one to accompany Him, except Peter and James and John the brother of James. **38** They came to the house of the synagogue official; and He saw a commotion, and people loudly weeping and wailing. **39** And entering in, He said to them, 'Why make a commotion and weep? The child has not died, but is asleep." **40** They began laughing at Him. But putting them all out, He took along the child's father and mother and His own companions, and entered the room where the child was. **41** Taking the child by the hand, He said to her, 'Talitha kum!' (which translated means, 'Little girl, I say to you, get up!'). **42** Immediately the girl got up and began to walk, for she was twelve years old. And immediately they were completely astounded. **43** And He gave them strict orders that no one should know about this, and He said that something should be given her to eat."

Matthew 9:27–31

"**27** As Jesus went on from there, two blind men followed Him, crying out, 'Have mercy on us, Son of David!' **28** When He entered the house, the blind men came up to Him, and Jesus said to them, 'Do you believe that I am able to do this?' They said to Him, 'Yes, Lord.' **29** Then He touched their eyes, saying, 'It shall be done to you according to your faith.' **30** And their eyes were opened. And Jesus sternly warned them: 'See that no one knows about this!' **31** But they went out and spread the news about Him throughout all that land."

1. When Jesus arrives at the shore on the other side of Galilee in verses 21–22, who does He encounter? What was his request of Jesus as Life Giver? (v. 23)

NOTE: The name Jairus means, "he will give light or awaken; enlighten."

2. Describe the scene in verse 24. Who enters the scene in verse 25? Read verses 25–26 out loud. Then record the details given about this new character.

3. Knowing the details of this woman's physical state, what do you think her emotional state might have been? Read Leviticus 15:25–35 for background.

4. What did the woman do and why in verses 27–28? What was the outcome? How do you think she might have felt in verse 29?

5. What was different about the woman's touch and the press of the crowd, as Jesus experienced it? What does the disciples' response in verse 31 suggest about their perspective?

6. How did the woman respond to Jesus' question in verse 33?

7. Jesus called the woman "daughter" in verse 34, the only time Scripture records Him ever using that term. What does that small yet powerful detail say to you about our life-giving Savior?

8. Jesus made three pronouncements over the woman. What were they?

9. There is a shift in tone in the scene in verse 35. What happened? What instruction did Jesus give the official in verse 36?

10. Who went to the house of Jairus and what did they find there? (see Amos 5:16 and Jeremiah 9:17)

11. What did Jesus say in verse 39 and how does this point to Him as Life Giver? What was the response in verse 40?

12. There is urgency and tension in this passage, yet we see many instances of Jesus' patience, compassion, and mercy. What is the message in Jesus' method?

13. Two men appear in Jesus' path in Matthew 9:27. What was their request and what did they call Jesus in verse 27? How did this demonstrate their "spiritual sight" was clear? (read God's covenant with David in 2 Samuel 7:16)

14. What question did Jesus ask the men in verse 28? What did Jesus acknowledge about the men in verse 29?

15. What did Jesus warn and how did they respond in verses 30–31?

Application

Have you ever experienced a physical condition that consumed your life, attention, or resources? How does this passage speak to you about God's love, power, and compassion for those who suffer physically? Do you believe Jesus is loving, powerful, and compassionate even if He does not heal?

A DEEPER LOOK

Review the stories of Jairus and the bleeding woman, who were both looking for help from Jesus in this passage. How are they alike? How are they different? What does each story illustrate about God's character?

How does this passage help illustrate Hebrews 11:6?

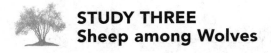

STUDY THREE
Sheep among Wolves

The disciples, along with many in Israel, had witnessed an abundance of life-changing miracles in recent days. Yet when Jesus stopped by His hometown, there was no ticker tape parade for the native Son. Instead, He was met with skepticism and resentment. "The hands of Jesus can build a table or stool, but not cast out demons, restore sight, and raise the dead!" These are the words of wolves, according to Jesus, and Israel's lost sheep living among them needed to receive His peace. So Jesus sent out the Twelve, His dear friends and followers, giving them authority to help and heal, but urging their continued dependence on the Father's provision. The commission came with clear warning: you will be rejected, despised, denounced and, in the end, even devoured. But all of it is for My sake, Jesus said, and for the sake of those I came to save. So be fearless and faithful, and the mission will be fruitful.

Mark 6:1–6
"Jesus went out from there and came into His hometown; and His disciples followed Him. ² When the Sabbath came, He began to teach in the synagogue; and the many listeners were astonished, saying, 'Where did this man get these things, and what is this wisdom given to Him, and such miracles as these performed by His hands? ³ Is not this the carpenter, the son of Mary, and brother of James and Joses and Judas and Simon? Are not His sisters here with us?' And they took

offense at Him. **4** Jesus said to them, 'A prophet is not without honor except in his hometown and among his own relatives and in his own household.' **5** And He could do no miracle there except that He laid His hands on a few sick people and healed them. **6** And He wondered at their unbelief.

And He was going around the villages teaching."

Matthew 10:5–23

"**5** These twelve Jesus sent out after instructing them: 'Do not go in the way of the Gentiles, and do not enter any city of the Samaritans; **6** but rather go to the lost sheep of the house of Israel. **7** And as you go, preach, saying, 'The kingdom of heaven is at hand.' **8** Heal the sick, raise the dead, cleanse the lepers, cast out demons. Freely you received, freely give. **9** Do not acquire gold, or silver, or copper for your money belts, **10** or a bag for your journey, or even two coats, or sandals, or a staff; for the worker is worthy of his support. **11** And whatever city or village you enter, inquire who is worthy in it, and stay at his house until you leave that city. **12** As you enter the house, give it your greeting. **13** If the house is worthy, give it your blessing of peace. But if it is not worthy, take back your blessing of peace. **14** Whoever does not receive you, nor heed your words, as you go out of that house or that city, shake the dust off your feet. **15** Truly I say to you, it will be more tolerable for the land of Sodom and Gomorrah in the day of judgment than for that city.

16 'Behold, I send you out as sheep in the midst of wolves; so be shrewd as serpents and innocent as doves. **17** But beware of men, for they will hand you over to the courts and scourge you in their synagogues; **18** and you will even be brought before governors and kings for My sake, as a testimony to them and to the Gentiles. **19** But when they hand you over, do not worry about how or what you are to say; for it will be given you in that hour what you are to say. **20** For it is not you who speak, but it is the Spirit of your Father who speaks in you.

21 'Brother will betray brother to death, and a father his child; and children will rise up against parents and cause them to be put to death. **22** You will be hated by all because of My name, but it is the one who has endured to the end who will be saved.

23 'But whenever they persecute you in one city, flee to the next; for truly I say to you, you will not finish going through the cities of Israel until the Son of Man comes."

1. What was the name of Jesus' hometown? (see Mark 1:9) What did Jesus do there and when? (Mark 6:2)

NOTE: The synagogue was the local meeting place where the Jews assembled and worshipped during New Testament times. Synagogues were implemented into the structure of Jewish culture after the temple was destroyed during the exile in 598 and 587 BC.

2. What questions did the people ask and how did they respond to Jesus? (vv. 2–3)

3. What do we learn about Jesus from Mark 6:3?

4. What is the meaning of Jesus' statement in Mark 6:4?

5. Based on this passage, what prevented Jesus from doing miracles among the people of His hometown?

6. We have seen Jesus "marvel" or be "amazed" (Matthew 8:10) before. At what does He marvel in Mark 6:6?

   Compare the two incidents that amazed Jesus.

7. Who is Jesus speaking to in verse 5? (see Matthew 10:1–4) What are they to do? What are they not to do? (vv. 5–14)

8. How are they to secure lodging? What are they to determine about the house? How are they to respond?

NOTE: The word "worthy" means someone who is willing and able to receive the teachings of Jesus.

9. What is the consequence for the city that does not receive the disciples (v. 15)?

10. How does Jesus set expectations for His disciples in verses 16–23 for this immediate and future ministry?

11. What posture does Jesus instruct the disciples to adopt in verse 16?

12. What are the trials they will endure? What are the blessings they will receive?

Application
How can we live "shrewd as serpents and innocent as doves" in the world today?

A DEEPER LOOK
Have you ever felt dishonored? How did you handle that? What does God's Word say about being honored?

Proverbs 15:33   Ephesians 6:1–3

Romans 12:10   Philippians 2:3

1 Corinthians 10:33   1 Peter 2:17–19

STUDY FOUR
Discipleship and Rewards

Jesus moved from commands and warnings to comfort and confidence as He instructed His disciples, reminding them that even when the enemy does his worst, they have a mightier Master. Their mission field was the fathers and mothers, sons and daughters of Israel, and their ministry was ordained by God. Persecution would be part of this work, but Jesus provided perspective: from birds in flight to the hairs on your head, the littlest things capture the Father's attention. And, there was promise of reward for those who offered even a cup of cold water to these men on a mission. So provision had been made in heaven and on earth. Jesus sent these men to love and serve, but they must love Him more or it's all for nothing. The time to take up their cross had come.

Matthew 10:24–11:1

"**24** 'A disciple is not above his teacher, nor a slave above his master. **25** It is enough for the disciple that he become like his teacher, and the slave like his master. If they have called the head of the house Beelzebub, how much more will they malign the members of his household!

26 'Therefore do not fear them, for there is nothing concealed that will not be revealed, or hidden that will not be known. **27** What I tell you in the darkness, speak in the light; and what you hear whispered in your ear, proclaim upon the housetops. **28** Do not fear those who kill the body but are unable to kill the soul; but rather fear Him who is able to destroy both soul and body in hell. **29** Are not two sparrows sold for a cent? And yet not one of them will fall to the ground apart from your Father. **30** But the very hairs of your head are all numbered. **31** So do not fear; you are more valuable than many sparrows.

32 'Therefore everyone who confesses Me before men, I will also confess him before My Father who is in heaven. **33** But whoever denies Me before men, I will also deny him before My Father who is in heaven.

34 'Do not think that I came to bring peace on the earth; I did not come to bring peace, but a sword. **35** For I came to set a man against his father, and a daughter against her mother, and a daughter-in-law against her mother-in-law; **36** and a man's enemies will be the members of his household.

37 'He who loves father or mother more than Me is not worthy of Me; and he who loves son or daughter more than Me is not worthy of Me. **38** And he who does not take his cross and follow after Me is not worthy of Me. **39** He who has found his life will lose it, and he who has lost his life for My sake will find it.

40 'He who receives you receives Me, and he who receives Me receives Him who sent Me. **41** He who receives a prophet in the name of a prophet shall receive a prophet's reward; and he who receives a righteous man in the name of a righteous man shall receive a righteous man's reward. **42** And whoever in the name of a disciple gives to one of these little ones even a cup of cold water to drink, truly I say to you, he shall not lose his reward.'

1 When Jesus had finished giving instructions to His twelve disciples, He departed from there to teach and preach in their cities."

1. What does Jesus say is the goal or aim of a disciple (vv. 24–25)?

2. What is the repeated command in verses 26–31? What is implied by Jesus' command about the heart of the disciples in this moment?

3. What comfort does Jesus give in this passage? What warning does Jesus give?

4. As you review this passage, what words of Jesus' might the disciples choose to remember and meditate on whenever they encounter opposition in their ministry?

5. What does it mean for the Prince of Peace (Isaiah 9:6) to speak the words in verses 34–39?

6. Who does Jesus say is worthy of Him? What is He saying about following Him? (vv. 37–39)

7. What is Jesus saying about discipleship in verse 38?

8. What is the difference between a person who "finds his life" and "loses his life" in verse 39? What does this mean?

9. What do verses 40–42 tell us about service done in the name and for the sake of Jesus?

10. Circle the word "reward" in verses 40–42. How are simple, obedient acts of service seen by the eyes of heaven?

11. What did Jesus do after He sent out His disciples? (11:1)

Application

Jesus spoke His call and commission to His disciples thousands of years ago. What can you take from His words today as a charge, comfort, challenge or correction?

STUDY FIVE
John's Fate Recalled

Sometimes it's hard to hear the truth, even when it would set you free. That was the tension between King Herod and John the Baptist — both men of influence, but only one on the side of right. John's words about willful sin and a coming Deliverer were equally fascinating and frightening to Herod. But in the end, fear prevailed. Herod's thoughtless vow to a manipulative girl became a death sentence for Jesus' cousin, and John's voice was silenced by the executioner's axe. The light of Jesus shone into the darkness of Herod's guilt, exposing his hard and deceived heart. Hatred for truth murdered a righteous and innocent man, proving John as Jesus' forerunner in life and in death.

Mark 6:14–29

"¹⁴ And King Herod heard of it, for His name had become well known; and people were saying, 'John the Baptist has risen from the dead, and that is why these miraculous powers are at work in Him.' ¹⁵ But others were saying, 'He is Elijah.' And others were saying, 'He is a prophet, like one of the prophets of old.' ¹⁶ But when Herod heard of it, he kept saying, 'John, whom I beheaded, has risen!'

¹⁷ For Herod himself had sent and had John arrested and bound in prison on account of Herodias, the wife of his brother Philip, because he had married her. ¹⁸ For John had been saying to Herod, 'It is not lawful for you to have your brother's wife.' ¹⁹ Herodias had a grudge against him and wanted to put him to death and could not do so; ²⁰ for Herod was afraid of John, knowing that he was a righteous and holy man, and he kept him safe. And when he heard him, he was very perplexed; but he used to enjoy listening to him. ²¹ A strategic day came when Herod on his birthday gave a banquet for his lords and military commanders and the leading men of Galilee; ²² and when the daughter of Herodias herself

came in and danced, she pleased Herod and his dinner guests; and the king said to the girl, 'Ask me for whatever you want and I will give it to you.' **23** And he swore to her, 'Whatever you ask of me, I will give it to you; up to half of my kingdom.' **24** And she went out and said to her mother, 'What shall I ask for?' And she said, 'The head of John the Baptist.' **25** Immediately she came in a hurry to the king and asked, saying, 'I want you to give me at once the head of John the Baptist on a platter.' **26** And although the king was very sorry, yet because of his oaths and because of his dinner guests, he was unwilling to refuse her. **27** Immediately the king sent an executioner and commanded him to bring back his head. And he went and had him beheaded in the prison, **28** and brought his head on a platter, and gave it to the girl; and the girl gave it to her mother. **29** When his disciples heard about this, they came and took away his body and laid it in a tomb."

1. Who is the subject of speculation in verses 14–16?

2. Why did King Herod think that Jesus was John?

3. Briefly summarize the story of John's death told in verses 17–28.

4. What was the sin John was speaking against? (vv. 17–18)

5. Describe Herod's relationship with John from the details in verse 20. What internal conflict did Herod have with regard to John? Why would the king be afraid of a prophet?

6. Why might Herodias' daughter have been in such a hurry in verse 25?

7. Why does Scripture say Herod did not want to break his word to Herodias' daughter? Why do you think he was "very sorry?" (v. 26)

8. What happened to John? What did his disciples do?

Application
Have you ever tried to silence God's voice in your life? Why? What was the result?

A DEEPER LOOK
Use a dictionary or biblestudytools.com to define the term *martyr*. What does the Bible say is in store in eternity for martyrs like John the Baptist?

Acts 7:54–60   Revelation 2:10

Romans 8:31–35   Revelation 6:9–11

2 Timothy 3:12   Revelation 20:4–5

1 Peter 4:14–16

WRAPPING UP

Whether it was with a touch or a word, Jesus lovingly gave life when all seemed lost. People came to Jesus seeking His power; their problems were severe and they had nowhere else to turn. They were seeking help for the here and now, but Jesus wanted to give them so much more.

We are all lost and dying without Him. The greatest gift He gives us is not health or happiness, but life—abundant life in Him today and for all eternity.

Reflect on the life-giving words Jesus speaks and the things Jesus does in this week's passages. Consider how you can speak and act in ways that are life giving to those around you.

—This is the end of Jesus' second year of ministry.

~ Map of Jesus in Capernaum ~

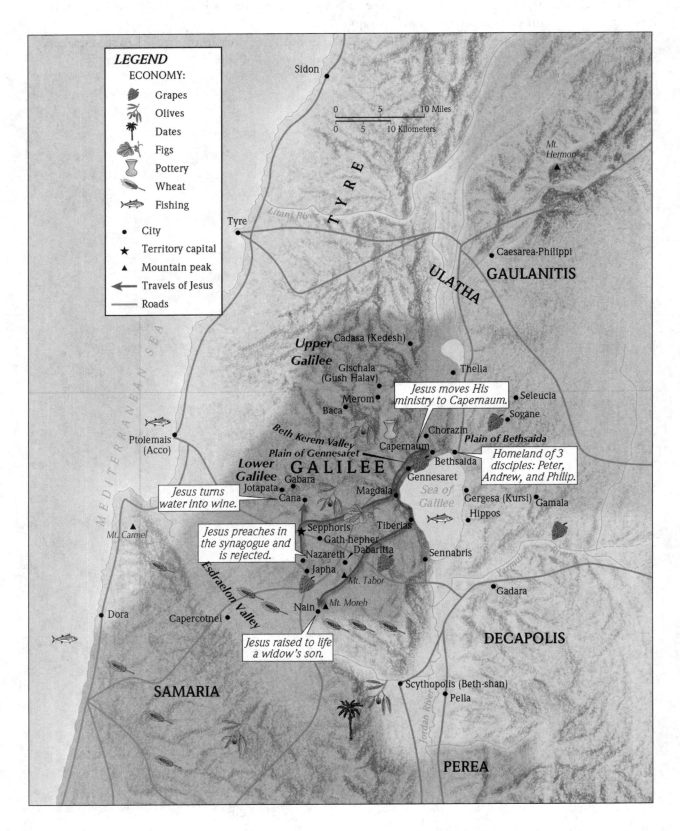

JESUS, THE BREAD OF LIFE

"Jesus said to them, 'I am the bread of life; he who comes to Me will not hunger, and he who believes in Me will never thirst.'"
JOHN 6:35

The multiplication of fish and loaves is the most famous calculation in history. And the math is mind blowing: Jesus used a little boy and his basket — a snack more than sustenance — to satisfy thousands whose hearts were full but stomachs empty. Jesus' miracle is still referenced today when we need to call to mind the possibility of creating magnitude from the miniscule.

Always relevant, Jesus called Himself "the Bread of Life" on the heels of this memorable meal. But that wasn't some half-baked political slogan or an homage to His power. Jesus knew the idea of food speaks to our most basic need. Like the hungry crowd in the desolate place, our bodies require physical nourishment to survive. While Jesus provided for their material needs, He was telling them — and us — He is so much more.

In His dialogue with the crowd, Jesus whets their appetites for the "true bread from heaven." It does not perish; it comes from a perfect place, and once you eat it you will never die. The people were on the edge of their seats, willing to pay any price for just a morsel.

Then Jesus laid it all on the table, inviting anyone who would come to the ultimate feast: *it's Me, He tells them. I'm the Living Bread, and I offer Myself as abundant life to this famished and wanting world.* For some, His claim was too much to take in. Others were eager for this spiritual Food, understanding Jesus gave life to body and soul.

STUDY ONE
Fish and Loaves and Walking on Water

With a broken heart and weary bones, Jesus sought refreshment in the presence of His Father. It was deep into the night when He decided to join His friends, and — as in most situations — Jesus used unconventional means. The sight of a Man walking on top of a turbulent sea had never been seen before. Jesus was unrecognizable at first, but the sound of His voice emboldened the impetuous Peter. So he stepped out toward Jesus, onto the rolling waves. Peter's trust and devotion moved him out of the boat and into a miracle, but distraction and fear weakened his faith. He began to sink, and Jesus saved him. Once back on board, the sea and their hearts were stilled. Jesus could have calmed the wind at any time, but He waited to see what His disciples would do. This time, they worshipped — unafraid and in awe of God's Son.

Matthew 14:13–36

"**13** Now when Jesus heard about John, He withdrew from there in a boat to a secluded place by Himself; and when the people heard of this, they followed Him on foot from the cities. **14** When He went ashore, He saw a large crowd, and felt compassion for them and healed their sick.

15 When it was evening, the disciples came to Him and said, 'This place is desolate and the hour is already late; so send the crowds away, that they may go into the villages and buy food for themselves.' **16** But Jesus said to them, 'They do not need to go away; you give them something to eat!' **17** They said to Him, 'We have here only five loaves and two fish.' **18** And He said, 'Bring them here to Me.' **19** Ordering the people to sit down on the grass, He took the five loaves and the two fish, and looking up toward heaven, He blessed the food, and breaking the loaves He gave them to the disciples, and the disciples gave them to the crowds, **20** and they all ate and were satisfied. They picked up what was left over of the broken pieces, twelve full baskets. **21** There were about five thousand men who ate, besides women and children.

22 Immediately He made the disciples get into the boat and go ahead of Him to the other side, while He sent the crowds away. **23** After He had sent the crowds away, He went up on the mountain by Himself to pray; and when it was evening, He was there alone. **24** But the boat was already a long distance from the land, battered by the waves; for the wind was contrary. **25** And in the fourth watch of the night He came to them, walking on the sea. **26** When the disciples saw Him walking on the sea, they were terrified, and said, 'It is a ghost!' And they cried out in fear. **27** But immediately Jesus spoke to them, saying, 'Take courage, it is I; do not be afraid.'

28 Peter said to Him, 'Lord, if it is You, command me to come to You on the water.' **29** And He said, 'Come!' And Peter got out of the boat, and walked on the water and came toward Jesus. **30** But seeing the wind, he became frightened, and beginning to sink, he cried out, 'Lord, save me!' **31** Immediately Jesus stretched out His hand and took hold of him, and said to him, 'You of little faith, why did you doubt?' **32** When they got into the boat, the wind stopped. **33** And those who were in the boat worshiped Him, saying, 'You are certainly God's Son!'

34 When they had crossed over, they came to land at Gennesaret. **35** And when the men of that place recognized Him, they sent word into all that surrounding district and brought to Him all who were sick; **36** and they implored Him that they might just touch the fringe of His cloak; and as many as touched it were cured."

1. What news did Jesus receive as this scene opens (see vv. 1–12)? How does Jesus respond to this news? What do His actions in verse 13 indicate about how He might be feeling? How does this display His humanity?

2. What is Jesus' response to the crowd in verse 14? How might His actions from verse 13 have prepared Him to engage?

3. What did the disciples want to do (v. 15)? What did Jesus tell the disciples to do? (vv. 16–17)

4. How did Jesus feed the people? What was His posture in prayer?

5. What details do you learn in verse 20? What does that tell you about God's provision?

6. What did Jesus do in verses 22–23? Why do you think He did that?

7. Describe the time of day and weather conditions in verses 24–25. What was Jesus doing in the midst of this scene?

NOTE: This is derived from a Roman method of keeping time, which was between 3 a.m. and 6 a.m.

8. Describe the disciples' state of mind in verse 26. What commands did Jesus give in verse 27?

9. What does Peter's statement in verse 28 say about him? What does it say about his relationship with Jesus?

10. An amazing miracle happens in verse 29 but quickly takes a turn in verse 30. What happened?

11. What word in verse 31 describes Jesus' response to Peter's cry for help? What did Jesus say was the reason Peter sank?

12. What was the response of those in the boat to Jesus (v. 33)? How does this compare to the last scene in a boat? (see Mark 4:41)

13. Where did Jesus and His disciples go next? How did the people respond to Him?

14. What detail related to healing the sick is expressed in verse 36? What is significant about that?

Application

When the disciples saw Jesus walking on the water, they were terrified—even though they had just experienced one of Jesus' greatest miracles: the feeding of the 5,000. What are some of the things that "frighten the faith" out of you?

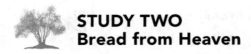 **STUDY TWO**
Bread from Heaven

Another day begins and the crowd once again seeks Jesus. How He arrived on the other side of the sea was a mystery that, at the time, only twelve men understood. But the reason the people were looking for Jesus was no secret at all. They were impressed with His power and wanted more of what He could give. But Jesus cared more about satisfying their souls than filling their stomachs. The words He spoke in this passage are controversial, just as they were to the hearers of the day. The vivid and violent images of eating flesh and drinking blood were offensive ideas to the religious Jews, but Jesus was speaking metaphorically—with the cross in mind and Himself as the final sacrifice. Bread baked in their earthen ovens grew stale over time and only sustained meal to meal. The Bread of Life would provide refreshment in a way they'd never known, and life they could know no other way.

John 6:22–58

"**22** The next day the crowd that stood on the other side of the sea saw that there was no other small boat there, except one, and that Jesus had not entered with His disciples into the boat, but that His disciples had gone away alone. **23** There came other small boats from Tiberias near to the place where they ate the bread after the Lord had given thanks. **24** So when the crowd saw that Jesus was not there, nor His disciples, they themselves got into the small boats, and came to Capernaum seeking Jesus. **25** When they found Him on the other side of the sea, they said to Him, 'Rabbi, when did You get here?'

26 Jesus answered them and said, 'Truly, truly, I say to you, you seek Me, not because you saw signs, but because you ate of the loaves and were filled. **27** Do not work for the food which perishes, but for the food which endures to eternal life, which the Son of Man will give to you, for on Him the Father, God, has set His seal.' **28** Therefore they said to Him, 'What shall we do, so that we may work the works of God?' **29** Jesus answered and said to them, 'This is the work of God, that you believe in Him whom He has sent.' **30** So they said to Him, 'What then do You do for a sign, so that we may see, and believe You? What work do You perform? **31** Our fathers ate the manna in the wilderness; as it is written, 'He gave them bread out of heaven to eat.' **32** Jesus then said to them, 'Truly, truly, I say to you, it is not Moses who has given you the bread out of heaven, but it is My Father who gives you the true bread out of heaven. **33** For the bread of God is that which comes down out of heaven, and gives life to the world.' **34** Then they said to Him, 'Lord, always give us this bread.'

35 Jesus said to them, 'I am the bread of life; he who comes to Me will not hunger, and he who believes in Me will never thirst. **36** But I said to you that you have seen Me, and yet do not believe. **37** All that the Father gives Me will come to Me, and the one who comes to Me I will certainly not cast out. **38** For I have come down from heaven, not to do My own will, but the will of Him who sent Me. **39** This is the will of Him who sent Me, that of all that He has given Me I lose nothing, but raise it up on the last day. **40** For this is the will of My Father, that everyone who beholds the Son and believes in Him will have eternal life, and I Myself will raise him up on the last day.'"

41 Therefore the Jews were grumbling about Him, because He said, 'I am the bread that came down out of heaven.' **42** They were saying, 'Is not this Jesus, the son of Joseph, whose father and mother we know? How does He now say, 'I have come down out of heaven'? **43** Jesus answered and said to them, 'Do not grumble among yourselves. **44** No one can come to Me unless the Father who sent Me draws him; and I will raise him up on the last day. **45** It is written in the prophets, 'And they shall all be taught of God.' Everyone who has heard and learned from the Father, comes to Me. **46** Not that anyone has seen the Father, except the One who is from God; He has seen the Father. **47** Truly, truly, I say to you, he who believes has eternal life. **48** I am the bread of life. **49** Your fathers ate the manna in the wilderness, and they died. **50** This is the bread which comes down out of heaven, so that one may eat of it and not die. **51** I am the living bread that came down out of heaven; if anyone eats of this bread, he will live forever; and the bread also which I will give for the life of the world is My flesh.'

52 Then the Jews began to argue with one another, saying, 'How can this man give us His flesh to eat?' **53** So Jesus said to them, 'Truly, truly, I say to you, unless you eat the flesh of the Son of Man and drink His blood, you have no life in your-selves. **54** He who eats My flesh and drinks My blood has eternal life, and I will raise him up on the last day. **55** For My flesh is true food, and My blood is true drink. **56** He who eats My flesh and drinks My blood abides in Me, and I in him. **57** As the living Father sent Me, and I live because of the Father, so he who eats Me, he also will live because of Me. **58** This is the bread which came down out of heaven; not as the fathers ate and died; he who eats this bread will live forever.'"

1. Why did the crowd pursue Jesus? (v. 26) Jesus is not speaking against work in verse 27. What is He exhorting the people to do?

2. Write down the question the people asked Jesus in verse 28. How does it appear the people define "work of God?" Compare that to Ephesians 2:8–10.

3. Write down Jesus' answer in verse 29. How does Jesus redefine "work of God" for the people?

4. Compare and contrast the language the people use in verses 30–31 with the words Jesus speaks in verses 32–33. Circle the actions words the people used. Underline the action words Jesus used.

5. What does Jesus say the "bread out of heaven" does in verse 33? What is ironic about the people's request in verse 34?

NOTE: Some translations more accurately replace "Lord" with "Sir" in verse 34 with respect to intent or attitude of the speakers.

6. What does Jesus proclaim about Himself in verse 35? What does He promise and to whom does He promise it in verses 35–40?

7. Based on Jesus' revelation of Himself in verse 35, what did Jesus mean in verse 27 when He said "seek the food that endures to eternal life?"

8. What is Jesus referring to when He says "all" in verses 37 and 39? Use verse 40 to help interpret.

9. Underline the phrase "out of heaven." (vv.41–58) How many times did Jesus repeat this? What was He trying to communicate?

10. What do verses 41–42 indicate was the Jews' problem with Jesus?

11. Read verses 37, 39–40, and 44–45. Who does Jesus say comes to the Father and how does faith play a role? (see Ephesians 2:8–9, 2 Peter 1:1, Philippians 1:29, Hebrews 12:2a)

12. What does Jesus say is the difference between the "bread" He offers and the manna of their ancestors in verses 48–51?

What does Jesus do for those who come to Him?

How does Jesus speak about our eternal security in Him as the Bread of Life?

13. What pivotal event in future history is Jesus referring to in verse 51?

14. In this challenging passage, Jesus continued to use a metaphor to illustrate what believing in Him looks like. Read verses 53–58 prayerfully and aloud. Substitute the word "believe(s) in" for "eat" and "drink." How does this help in your understanding of the passage?

Application
Like the people and their preconceived notion of Joseph's Son, how willing are you to give someone a second chance or fresh start? Have you ever been judged based on your background, your past, or your family?

A DEEPER LOOK
The idea of consuming blood was offensive to the Jews and forbidden by the Law (Leviticus 7:26–27). Yet Jesus was making an important point about His future sacrifice. Read these verses and observe why the blood of Jesus is crucial to salvation.

Romans 5:9   Hebrews 9:12, 22

Ephesians 1:7   1 John 1:7

Ephesians 2:13   Revelation 5:9–10

Colossians 1:20

STUDY THREE
Confession of Faith

Teaching that is hard to hear is not necessarily wrong. Our ability to wrap our minds around something difficult does not make it more or less true. Such is the case for Jesus and the Jews. To some, Jesus' words were challenging at least; others claimed this was heresy at its worst. But Jesus wasn't going to soften or repackage the truth to make His message easier to digest. Instead of wrestling through it, many who had been walking with Him simply walked away. His demonstrations of deity—the signs they longed for, the healing they needed—weren't enough after all. Only those with teachable hearts and faith from above would continue on this road. In asking a question of commitment, Jesus gave the Twelve a chance to either stand with the crowd or out from it. They chose to stand firmly with Him.

John 6:59–71

"⁵⁹ These things He said in the synagogue as He taught in Capernaum.

⁶⁰ Therefore many of His disciples, when they heard this said, 'This is a difficult statement; who can listen to it?' ⁶¹ But Jesus, conscious that His disciples grumbled at this, said to them, 'Does this cause you to stumble? ⁶² What then if you see the Son of Man ascending to where He was before? ⁶³ It is the Spirit who gives life; the flesh profits nothing; the words that I have spoken to you are spirit and are life. ⁶⁴ But there are some of you who do not believe.' For Jesus knew from the beginning who they were who did not believe, and who it was that would betray Him. ⁶⁵ And He was saying, 'For this reason I have said to you, that no one can come to Me unless it has been granted him from the Father.'

⁶⁶ As a result of this many of His disciples withdrew and were not walking with Him anymore. ⁶⁷ So Jesus said to the twelve, 'You do not want to go away also, do you?' ⁶⁸ Simon Peter answered Him, 'Lord, to whom shall we go? You have words of eternal life. ⁶⁹ We have believed and have come to know that You are the Holy One of God.' ⁷⁰ Jesus answered them, 'Did I Myself not choose you, the twelve, and yet one of you is a devil?' ⁷¹ Now He meant Judas the son of Simon Iscariot, for he, one of the twelve, was going to betray Him."

1. Where does this scene take place (v. 59)?

2. What is the evidence in this passage that Jesus' teaching was hard to hear, understand, and follow? What about the teaching we examined in Study Two would have been difficult for the disciples?

3. Their resistance to Jesus' teaching actually proves Jesus' point. Read and review verses 44, 63, 64–65, 67–69. What is the difference between those who continue to follow Jesus and those who turned back?

4. Where do we see Jesus' sovereignty on display in this passage?

5. How do Peter's words to Jesus in verses 68–69 encourage you?

6. What does Judas' presence among the chosen Twelve say to us? How is God sovereign in the choosing of Judas as a disciple and in His betrayal?

7. What evidence do we see in this passage that Jesus' teaching was a stumbling block to some and a stepping stone to others?

Application
The people said they found Jesus' teaching difficult. What are some truths from God's Word that are hard for you? How do you submit to them?

A DEEPER LOOK

What does the Bible say about grumbling? How does God feel about grumbling, whether spoken or in our hearts?

Numbers 14:26–30   Ephesians 4:29

Ecclesiastes 10:20   Philippians 2:14

1 Corinthians 10:8–11   James 5:9

STUDY FOUR
Tradition and Teaching

Jesus moved the conversation from "intake" to "output" as the Pharisees provided the perfect example of faithless words emerging from hypocritical hearts. Once again, Jesus established a holy hierarchy from heaven that overthrew the empty, self-important traditions of the Jews. The way you speak is more important than what you eat, Jesus told them, and your words must be filtered through a pure heart. Washing your hands does nothing to clean you up inside. Sin permeates to the core and can't be removed by mere ritual. With her words, the Gentile woman demonstrated humble faith in Jesus and right understanding of her position. She threw herself on His mercy and waited, confident He would act. The result? Healing for her child and honor from her Lord.

Matthew 15:1–28
"Then some Pharisees and scribes came to Jesus from Jerusalem and said, **2** 'Why do Your disciples break the tradition of the elders? For they do not wash their hands when they eat bread.' **3** And He answered and said to them, 'Why do you yourselves transgress the commandment of God for the sake of your tradition? **4** For God said, 'Honor your father and mother,' and, 'He who speaks evil of

father or mother is to be put to death.' **5** But you say, 'Whoever says to his father or mother, 'Whatever I have that would help you has been given to God,' **6** he is not to honor his father or his mother.' And by this you invalidated the word of God for the sake of your tradition. **7** You hypocrites, rightly did Isaiah prophesy of you:

8 'This people honors Me with their lips,
But their heart is far away from Me.
9 'But in vain do they worship Me,
Teaching as doctrines the precepts of men.'

10 After Jesus called the crowd to Him, He said to them, 'Hear and understand. **11** It is not what enters into the mouth that defiles the man, but what proceeds out of the mouth, this defiles the man.'

12 Then the disciples came and said to Him, 'Do You know that the Pharisees were offended when they heard this statement?' **13** But He answered and said, 'Every plant which My heavenly Father did not plant shall be uprooted. **14** Let them alone; they are blind guides of the blind. And if a blind man guides a blind man, both will fall into a pit.'

15 Peter said to Him, 'Explain the parable to us.' **16** Jesus said, 'Are you still lacking in understanding also? **17** Do you not understand that everything that goes into the mouth passes into the stomach, and is eliminated? **18** But the things that proceed out of the mouth come from the heart, and those defile the man. **19** For out of the heart come evil thoughts, murders, adulteries, fornications, thefts, false witness, slanders. **20** These are the things which defile the man; but to eat with unwashed hands does not defile the man.'

21 Jesus went away from there, and withdrew into the district of Tyre and Sidon. **22** And a Canaanite woman from that region came out and began to cry out, saying, 'Have mercy on me, Lord, Son of David; my daughter is cruelly demon-possessed.' **23** But He did not answer her a word. And His disciples came and implored Him, saying, 'Send her away, because she keeps shouting at us.' **24** But He answered and said, 'I was sent only to the lost sheep of the house of Israel.' **25** But she came and began to bow down before Him, saying, 'Lord, help me!' **26** And He answered and said, 'It is not good to take the children's bread and throw it to the dogs.' **27** But she said, 'Yes, Lord; but even the dogs feed on the crumbs which fall from their masters' table.' **28** Then Jesus said to her, 'O woman, your faith is great; it shall be done for you as you wish.' And her daughter was healed at once."

1. Where was Jesus in this passage? (see Matthew 14:34) Who came to Jesus? Where did they come from? What did they want to know?

2. What example of a "tradition of the elders" did those men provide (v. 2)?

3. Read verses 3–6 out loud. Write in your own words (summarize) Jesus' response to their accusations.

NOTE:

Read Mark 7:11 as a parallel verse to Matthew 15:5. "Corban" is a gift or offering consecrated to God. The Pharisees expanded their own authority and replaced the original intent with a convenient tradition: they allowed for continued use of the object (food, property) while at the same time exempting themselves from sharing with others.

4. What does it mean to have "invalidated the Word of God" (v. 6)? How are the religious leaders "hypocrites," as diagnosed by Jesus in verse 7?

5. How do Isaiah's words in verses 8–9 bring insight to this exchange?

6. What did Jesus want the crowds to "hear and understand" in verse 10?

7. Why do you think the disciples said what they did to Jesus in verse 12? What does it reveal about them?

8. In verse 13, what is the "plant?" How does the Father "plant" and what is the result if He doesn't?

9. What kind of guides or leaders were the Pharisees (v. 14)? How were the highly educated, wealthy, socially prominent, and extremely religious people "blind?"

10. What does Jesus say defiles a man (vv. 11, 18–19)? How was this different from what the religious leaders taught? (v. 20)

11. Who did Jesus encounter in Tyre and Sidon? What was her need? How did she address Jesus? What does this indicate? What was Jesus' unusual response? (vv. 21–23)

12. What did the disciples want to do? What was Jesus' explanation? (vv. 23–24)

13. Thinking big picture, what is the purpose of placing the story of the Syrophoenician woman (Canaanite) immediately after their discussion about purity of the heart?

14. What is the difference between the disciples' understanding of Jesus' parables (verses 15–16) and the woman's understanding of Jesus' parables (verses 26–27)? What difference does Jesus note in verse 28? What do you observe was "great" about this woman's faith? What was the result for the woman's daughter?

15. How do you see the grace of God on display in this passage?

Application

Do you ever hesitate to bring a need to the Lord because you feel like a child interrupting an important and busy Father? How does the story of the Syrophoenician woman encourage and instruct you?

What are some traditions that are important to you and your family? What are some examples of church traditions?

Do you know the difference between a tradition and a commandment from God? What is an example in our spiritual lives of a tradition being mistaken for a command or a commandment being wrongly viewed as an optional tradition?

> **NOTE:** The Lord's Supper and baptism are ordinances or commands from Scripture rather than man-made traditions.

STUDY FIVE
Healing and Feeding Crowds

Jesus gave His disciples a gift in allowing them to witness a great contrast: the doubt of the unbelieving religious Jews and the confident faith of the Gentile woman. Jesus had come first for Israel's lost sheep, but we see He was equally stirred by the hurts of the wider world. They remained in the Gentile region where Jesus freely healed and restored. His miracles were fueled by compassion for these people who were "far off," and their response to Him was pure worship. Jesus fed this multitude of outsiders on the east side of the Sea just as He did the Jews only days before. What is almost more mind-boggling this time is the disciples' lack of memory. Jesus provided an opportunity for His friends to exercise their faith, and they faltered. But Jesus never does, and once again, everyone was satisfied by the Bread of Life.

Matthew 15:29–39
"**29** Departing from there, Jesus went along by the Sea of Galilee, and having gone up on the mountain, He was sitting there. **30** And large crowds came to Him, bringing with them those who were lame, crippled, blind, mute, and many others, and they laid them down at His feet; and He healed them. **31** So the crowd marveled as they saw the mute speaking, the crippled restored, and the lame walking, and the blind seeing; and they glorified the God of Israel.

32 And Jesus called His disciples to Him, and said, 'I feel compassion for the people, because they have remained with Me now three days and have nothing to eat; and I do not want to send them away hungry, for they might faint on the way." **33** The disciples said to Him, 'Where would we get so many loaves in this desolate place to satisfy such a large crowd?' **34** And Jesus said to them, 'How many loaves do you have?' And they said, 'Seven, and a few small fish.' **35** And He directed the people to sit down on the ground; **36** and He took the seven loaves and the fish; and giving thanks, He broke them and started giving them to the disciples, and the disciples gave them to the people. **37** And they all ate and were satisfied, and they picked up what was left over of the broken pieces, seven large baskets full. **38** And those who ate were four thousand men, besides women and children.

39 And sending away the crowds, Jesus got into the boat and came to the region of Magadan."

1. Where did Jesus go next in verse 29?

2. The scene is written simply, but the content is profound. Take a moment to read verses 29–31 thoughtfully and picture it in your mind.

   • Who did the "large crowds" bring to Jesus?

   • What did Jesus do?

   • How did the crowd respond?

3. Read the parallel passage of Mark 7:31–8:10. It indicates this healing and feeding took place in a Gentile region of Galilee. What does this say about the ministry of the Bread of Life? What evidence in verse 31 shows the crowd connected Jesus the Son to God the Father?

4. What is the situation as Jesus described it in verse 32?

5. Jesus healed and then filled the crowd. How many people does verse 38 tell us are fed in this scene?

6. Review Matthew 14:13–21. What is familiar about this scene? What is different?

Application

We marvel at the disciples' lack of faith and short-term memory loss on display in verse 33. How could they so quickly forget the way the Bread of Life has provided in the past? And yet we are the same! What are some ways God has been faithful to meet your needs? How quick are you to praise Him for doing so?

WRAPPING UP

Break down the metaphor of eating and drinking, and consider how our senses can help in our understanding of our relationship with Jesus, the Bread of Life. Think about what food and drink provide for us, and how necessary they are to our survival. We can't just stock our fridge and think that's enough. We must consume the sustenance within in order to live. And there is even more blessing: God has enabled us to enjoy the things we eat and drink. We can take delight in what we consume and even become stronger and healthier because of it!

When we stop and prayerfully digest this image, we can begin to grasp the real necessity and pure joy of Jesus! *O taste and see that the Lord is good!* (Psalms 34:8)

~ Map of Peter's Confession ~

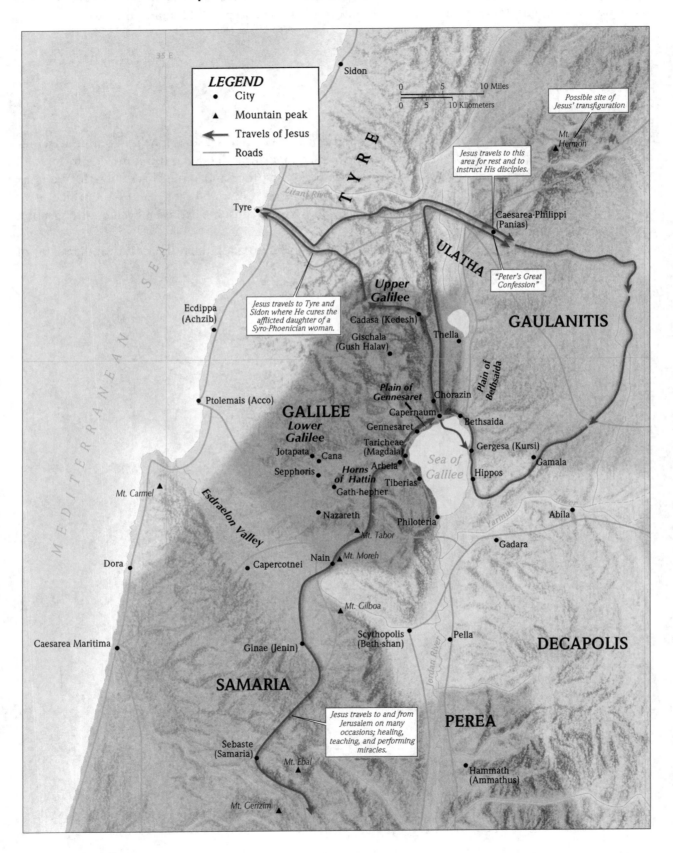

Legend
- • City
- ▲ Mountain peak
- ← Travels of Jesus
- — Roads

35 E

Sidon

0   5   10 Miles
0   5   10 Kilometers

Possible site of Jesus' transfiguration

▲ Mt. Hermon

TYRE

Litani River

Jesus travels to this area for rest and to instruct His disciples.

Tyre

Caesarea-Philippi (Panias)

ULATHA

"Peter's Great Confession"

Ecdippa (Achzib)

Jesus travels to Tyre and Sidon where He cures the afflicted daughter of a Syro-Phoenician woman.

Upper Galilee

Cadasa (Kedesh)

Gischala (Gush Halav)

Thella

GAULANITIS

M E D I T E R R A N E A N   S E A

Ptolemais (Acco)

Plain of Gennesaret

Chorazin

Plain of Bethsaida

GALILEE
Lower Galilee

Capernaum

Gennesaret

Bethsaida

Jotapata   Cana

Taricheae (Magdala)

Gergesa (Kursi)

Gamala

Sepphoris

Horns of Hattin

Arbela

Sea of Galilee

Hippos

Gath-hepher

Tiberias

▲ Mt. Carmel

Esdraelon Valley

Abila

Nazareth

▲ Mt. Tabor

Philoteria

Yarmuk

Dora

Capercotnei

Nain ▲ Mt. Moreh

Gadara

▲ Mt. Gilboa

SAMARIA

Caesarea Maritima

Ginae (Jenin)

Scythopolis (Beth-shan)

Pella

Jordan River

DECAPOLIS

PEREA

Jesus travels to and from Jerusalem on many occasions; healing, teaching, and performing miracles.

Sebaste (Samaria)

▲ Mt. Ebal

Hammath (Ammathus)

▲ Mt. Gerizim

JESUS, SON OF GOD

*"While he was still speaking, a bright cloud overshadowed them,
and behold, a voice out of the cloud said, 'This is My beloved Son,
with whom I am well-pleased; listen to Him!'"*

MATTHEW 17:5

J esus was called Teacher, Master, and Lord by some, and accused of being an agent of Beelzebub by others. The name "Jesus" was on the lips of everyone in Israel, but His real identity was muddied by the misconceptions of the masses. When faith was given full reign, their vision of Jesus was clear. But creeping doubt often clouded the truth and led them to stumble.

Caesarea Philippi, crammed with dark deities, was the background against which faith shone light on the true nature of Jesus. It was no mistake that Peter proclaimed Jesus the "Son of God" in one of the most idolatrous regions in the history of Israel. And not just any god—the one true *living* God, distinct from and exalted above all that their eyes could see.

This declaration was not about divine *pater familias*; God the Father did not have a Son in the way human families are formed. God so loved the world that He gave His only Son, manifested in the flesh as Jesus. Jesus came into the world by the work of the Holy Spirit through His earthly mother, Mary. As the Son of God, Jesus was—in His essence and existence—the same as God. And the Son is our Savior.

This was blasphemy to the unbelieving Jews, who were threatened and confused by this design. And that is why they called for Jesus' death. The only One that Jesus was living to please was His Father, and on a high mountain with the past and future looking on, God Himself echoed the proclamation of Peter: You are in the presence of the Son of God—lift up your eyes and worship!

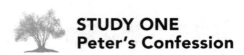

STUDY ONE
Peter's Confession

The healing of the blind man was the perfect picture of the disciples' progressing spiritual sight. When he first met Jesus, the man was consumed by darkness. Jesus was capable of completely healing any affliction, but His touch this time purposely had only partial effect. The man's sight was emerging but blurry until Jesus touched his eyes again, giving his world clarity and light. Such was the case for the disciples, who had lived each day in the presence of the Son. They mostly saw Jesus dimly until, in a city filled with false gods, heaven's light opened Peter's eyes to the living, breathing Truth. But it only takes one wrong step to fall from the height of insight into shortsighted, stubborn sin. Peter quickly discovered rocks can crumble, but the rubble will be redeemed.

Mark 8:22–26

"22 And they came to Bethsaida. And they brought a blind man to Jesus and implored Him to touch him. 23 Taking the blind man by the hand, He brought him out of the village; and after spitting on his eyes and laying His hands on him, He asked him, 'Do you see anything?' 24 And he looked up and said, 'I see men, for I see them like trees, walking around.' 25 Then again He laid His hands on his eyes; and he looked intently and was restored, and began to see everything clearly. 26 And He sent him to his home, saying, 'Do not even enter the village.'"

Matthew 16:13–23

"13 Now when Jesus came into the district of Caesarea Philippi, He was asking His disciples, 'Who do people say that the Son of Man is?' 14 And they said, 'Some say John the Baptist; and others, Elijah; but still others, Jeremiah, or one of the prophets.' 15 He said to them, 'But who do you say that I am?' 16 Simon Peter answered, 'You are the Christ, the Son of the living God.' 17 And Jesus said to him, 'Blessed are you, Simon Barjona, because flesh and blood did not reveal this to you, but My Father who is in heaven. 18 I also say to you that you are Peter, and upon this rock I will build My church; and the gates of Hades will not overpower it. 19 I will give you the keys of the kingdom of heaven; and whatever you bind on earth shall have been bound in heaven, and whatever you loose on earth shall have been loosed in heaven.' 20 Then He warned the disciples that they should tell no one that He was the Christ.

21 From that time Jesus began to show His disciples that He must go to Jerusalem, and suffer many things from the elders and chief priests and scribes, and be killed, and be raised up on the third day. 22 Peter took Him aside and began to rebuke Him, saying, 'God forbid it, Lord! This shall never happen to You.' 23 But He turned and said to Peter, 'Get behind Me, Satan! You are a stumbling block to Me; for you are not setting your mind on God's interests, but man's.'"

1. Where is Jesus? Who came to Jesus and what was the request?

2. Where did Jesus take the man (see Matthew 11:21–22)?

Describe how this man was healed.

3. What is different about this healing miracle compared to other stories?

4. The healing of the blind man is a living parable or illustration for the disciples. What is Jesus communicating to them about their faith and relationship with Him?

5. Circle the verbs in verses 24–25 that point to the man's experience/participation in his healing. What warning did Jesus give him? (v. 26)

6. Read Psalms 146:8, Isaiah 29:18, and Isaiah 35:5–6. For anyone familiar with the Old Testament and witnessing this event, what could they conclude about Jesus?

7. Where was Jesus in Matthew 16:13? What two questions did He ask and of whom did He ask them? (vv.13, 15)

8. What does verse 14 reveal about the people's understanding of Jesus? What obvious option is missing from their "list?"

9. Who answers Jesus' second question in verse 16? What did he say?

10. What did Jesus say about Peter, his answer, and the future of God's kingdom in verses 17–19?

NOTE: This is the first mention of the word and concept of "church" in the New Testament.

11. To whom does Jesus say the church belongs in verse 18? What protection does Jesus promise in verse 18? How does that encourage you?

12. Read Acts 2:36–41 and Acts 10:34–45. Record how Peter used the "keys" to open the kingdom of heaven to Jews and Gentiles.

13. In verse 19 of Matthew, to help in interpretation, substitute the word "forbid" for the word "bind" and the word "allow" for the word "loose." What form does that kind of governing authority take in churches today? Where does their authority come from? (see Acts 20:17–38; 1 Timothy 3:1–13; Titus 1:6–9; 1 Peter 5:1–4)

14. Why do you think Jesus said what he did in verse 20? Could Jesus' warning be connected to the information about the people in verse 14? In what way?

15. Verse 21 marks a shift in the ministry of Jesus. What does Matthew say Jesus began to do with His disciples?

16. What is the order of events as described by Jesus in verse 21? Who are the three groups Jesus said would be a part of His suffering?

17. How did Peter respond to this new information about the earthly ministry of Jesus? What do the words "began to rebuke" in verse 22 indicate about how this conversation unfolded?

18. What did Jesus call Peter? Why did He call him that? What does Jesus say in verse 23 was the reason for Peter's misunderstanding of Jesus' purpose on earth?

19. How does Jesus' response to Peter's rebuke show Jesus' humanity? (see Matthew 4:8–11)

Application

Use one or two adjectives to describe your spiritual growth over the past year and over the past five to ten years. How has God "healed" you "in phases?" (1 Corinthians 13:12; 1 John 3:12)

A DEEPER LOOK

There have been many interpretations through history about the identity of the "rock" in verse 18. Read the verses below and identify what Scripture refers to as "rock" or "stone."

Psalms 118:22   1 Corinthians 3:11, 10:4

Isaiah 28:16   Ephesians 2:20–21

Acts 4:10–12   1 Peter 2:4–5

STUDY TWO
The Transfiguration

It is hard to give up a self-gratifying life here and now for the promise of an eternally gratifying one. C.S. Lewis called this upside down way of living the chance to "die before you die." When Jesus told His disciples that following Him meant denying self, He wasn't talking about saying "no" to dessert or working harder to have a quiet time. He meant it was time to trade in their personal Bill of Rights for a promissory note of future glory. Jesus knew that true joy comes when we realize we are unfit to rule ourselves and humbly submit to His loving authority over our lives. Peter, James, and John got a glimpse of this glory on a mountaintop as they witnessed Jesus' earthly body supernaturally transformed to reflect His true self. Peter wanted to preserve the moment, but the Father intervened with a better plan. God knew all that was to come, and commanded the men to listen to the One who would lead them.

Matthew 16:24–17:13

"24 Then Jesus said to His disciples, 'If anyone wishes to come after Me, he must deny himself, and take up his cross and follow Me. 25 For whoever wishes to save his life will lose it; but whoever loses his life for My sake will find it. 26 For what will it profit a man if he gains the whole world and forfeits his soul? Or what will a man give in exchange for his soul? 27 For the Son of Man is going to come in the glory of His Father with His angels, and will then repay every man according to his deeds.

28 'Truly I say to you, there are some of those who are standing here who will not taste death until they see the Son of Man coming in His kingdom.'"

1 Six days later Jesus took with Him Peter and James and John his brother, and led them up on a high mountain by themselves. 2 And He was transfigured before them; and His face shone like the sun, and His garments became as white as light. 3 And behold, Moses and Elijah appeared to them, talking with Him. 4 Peter said to Jesus, 'Lord, it is good for us to be here; if You wish, I will make three tabernacles here, one for You, and one for Moses, and one for Elijah.' 5 While he was still speaking, a bright cloud overshadowed them, and behold, a voice out of the cloud said, 'This is My beloved Son, with whom I am well-pleased; listen to Him!' 6 When the disciples heard this, they fell face down to the ground and were terrified. 7 And Jesus came to them and touched them and said, 'Get up, and do not be afraid.' 8 And lifting up their eyes, they saw no one except Jesus Himself alone.

9 As they were coming down from the mountain, Jesus commanded them, saying, 'Tell the vision to no one until the Son of Man has risen from the dead.' 10 And His disciples asked Him, 'Why then do the scribes say that Elijah must come first?' 11 And He answered and said, 'Elijah is coming and will restore all things; 12 but I say to you that Elijah already came, and they did not recognize him, but did to him whatever they wished. So also the Son of Man is going to suffer at their hands.' 13 Then the disciples understood that He had spoken to them about John the Baptist."

1. Jesus explains the cost and rewards of following Him in verses 24–28. What are the costs? What are the rewards?

> NOTE: Jesus mentions the cross here to the disciples for the first time. No one but Jesus was yet aware of how He would die.

2. How is verse 16:28 connected to verse 17:1–2?

3. Who did Jesus take up with Him on the mountain? (v. 1) Briefly describe what happens in this scene. See Luke 9:28–31 for more details. Define "transfiguration" using the dictionary or www.biblestudy-tools.com.

4. What does Luke 9:31 tell us Jesus and His companions were discussing?

5. What was Peter planning in verse 4? Who interrupts Peter in verse 5? What declaration and instruction was given?

6. How did the disciples respond? (v. 6) How could this experience help fortify these men to obey Jesus' previous command in vv. 24–27?

7. Who was Moses? Who was Elijah? Why do you think they appeared with Jesus?

8. What were the disciples supposed to do with the vision they were shown (v. 9)?

9. What did the disciples say was the "popular opinion" of the day in verse 10? How did Jesus correct that?

Application
There was a cost for the disciples to follow Jesus. What is He calling you to give up and what is the cost? What is the reward?

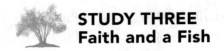

STUDY THREE
Faith and a Fish

The unbelief of the disciples is tied to an inadequate faith that failed to aid a father and his demon-possessed son. The disciples' commission in Matthew 10 came with power, but it wasn't meant to be used like a pill, taken only when needed. Jesus was looking for their constant dependence on Him, a continual reliance that could move mountains on command. An ongoing walk would allow for a deeper revelation of Himself and God's plan and build trust that could turn their grief into joy as deep as the sea. It took that kind of faith for Peter to walk to the edge of the water and believe he would hook a shekel instead of a sardine. Jesus used Peter to obtain the temple tribute in a way only He could, avoiding offense by miraculous means.

Matthew 17:14–27

"**14** When they came to the crowd, a man came up to Jesus, falling on his knees before Him and saying, **15** 'Lord, have mercy on my son, for he is a lunatic and is very ill; for he often falls into the fire and often into the water. **16** I brought him to Your disciples, and they could not cure him.' **17** And Jesus answered and said, 'You unbelieving and perverted generation, how long shall I be with you? How long shall I put up with you? Bring him here to Me.' **18** And Jesus rebuked him, and the demon came out of him, and the boy was cured at once.

19 Then the disciples came to Jesus privately and said, 'Why could we not drive it out?' **20** And He said to them, 'Because of the littleness of your faith; for truly I say to you, if you have faith the size of a mustard seed, you will say to this mountain, 'Move from here to there,' and it will move; and nothing will be impossible to you. **21** [But this kind does not go out except by prayer and fasting.']

22 And while they were gathering together in Galilee, Jesus said to them, 'The Son of Man is going to be delivered into the hands of men; **23** and they will kill Him, and He will be raised on the third day.' And they were deeply grieved.

24 When they came to Capernaum, those who collected the two-drachma tax came to Peter and said, 'Does your teacher not pay the two-drachma tax?' **25** He said, 'Yes.' And when he came into the house, Jesus spoke to him first, saying, 'What do you think, Simon? From whom do the kings of the earth collect customs or poll-tax, from their sons or from strangers?' **26** When Peter said, 'From strangers,' Jesus said to him, 'Then the sons are exempt. **27** However, so that we do not offend them, go to the sea and throw in a hook, and take the first fish that comes up; and when you open its mouth, you will find a shekel. Take that and give it to them for you and Me.'"

1. What happened when Jesus and the disciples reentered reality in verse 14?

2. What was the problem (vv. 15–16)? What was the cause (v. 18)?

3. What explanation did Jesus provide for the disciples regarding their powerlessness over the demon? (v. 20)

4. What was the difference between the disciples' "little" faith that was ineffective and the "little" mustard-seed faith that can move mountains?

5. Where did the disciples' power to heal come from according to Luke 9:1–2 and Mark 6:7? How might acknowledging that fact have affected their power to heal and their amount of faith?

6. What did Jesus promise would happen in verses 22–23? What evidence do we see that the disciples seemed to grasp His proclamation?

7. Where were Jesus and His disciples in verse 24?

8. How did Jesus display His omniscience in this story?

NOTE: The temple tax comes from Exodus 30:11–16. This tax was established to help pay for the maintenance and services of the temple. This was a Jewish tax on the Jewish people rather than a Roman tax imposed on the Jews.

9. Since this is a temple tax, who is the "King" of the temple? Who is His Son?

10. What conclusion did the Son of God draw in verse 26 from this logic? How did Jesus choose to respond instead and why (v. 27)?

11. What miracle took place to provide the tax? How would the means of provision been particularly meaningful to Peter?

12. What was required of Peter to obey Jesus' strange command in verse 27?

Application

What are some decisions you make in life and in relationships in order to keep from needlessly offending others? Why is this important?

STUDY FOUR
Stumbling Blocks, Stepping Stones

Humility was the stumbling block here for the disciples, who sought status in the kingdom of heaven. Rather than pointing to a mighty warrior or royal lineage, Jesus offered a little child as the best example of a citizen of the kingdom. Jesus upended greatness with a living example of how childlike faith surpasses conceited self-sufficiency every time. Jesus was also serious about not obstructing the faith of others. Rejecting Jesus had its own perils, but there is also a heavy price for anyone who causes another to turn away from Him. For the sheep who do wander, Jesus said He'd leave everything behind to restore even one to His flock. And their return brings Him extraordinary joy.

Matthew 18:1–14
"At that time the disciples came to Jesus and said, 'Who then is greatest in the kingdom of heaven?' 2 And He called a child to Himself and set him before them, 3 and said, 'Truly I say to you, unless you are converted and become like children, you will not enter the kingdom of heaven. 4 Whoever then humbles himself as this child, he is the greatest in the kingdom of heaven. 5 And whoever receives one such child in My name receives Me; 6 but whoever causes one of these little ones who believe in Me to stumble, it would be better for him to have a heavy millstone hung around his neck, and to be drowned in the depth of the sea.

7 'Woe to the world because of its stumbling blocks! For it is inevitable that stumbling blocks come; but woe to that man through whom the stumbling block comes!

8 'If your hand or your foot causes you to stumble, cut it off and throw it from you; it is better for you to enter life crippled or lame, than to have two hands or two feet and be cast into the eternal fire. **9** If your eye causes you to stumble, pluck it out and throw it from you. It is better for you to enter life with one eye, than to have two eyes and be cast into the fiery hell.

10 'See that you do not despise one of these little ones, for I say to you that their angels in heaven continually see the face of My Father who is in heaven. **11** [For the Son of Man has come to save that which was lost.]

12 'What do you think? If any man has a hundred sheep, and one of them has gone astray, does he not leave the ninety-nine on the mountains and go and search for the one that is straying? **13** If it turns out that he finds it, truly I say to you, he rejoices over it more than over the ninety-nine which have not gone astray. **14** So it is not the will of your Father who is in heaven that one of these little ones perish."

1. Take a minute to review the timeline of events since Peter's confession of Christ at Caesarea Philippi in Matthew 16:16. Write a brief chronology below.

2. What did the disciples want to know in 18:1? Based on the context of the timeline, what does their question expose about the disciples? What sort of kingdom do you think they meant?

3. Jesus could have pointed to Himself as the answer to this question. Who does He point to instead? Why does He do this? How does this example illustrate Jesus' point? (vv. 2–3)

NOTE: Other translations use the words "turn," "change," or "turn around," instead of "are converted" in verse 3.

4. Jesus was not saying children are perfect or innocent (see Ecclesiastes 7:20, Romans 3:10, and Romans 3:23). So what character traits do children possess that Jesus could have been pointing the disciples toward?

5. What was Jesus' description of greatness? How was that different from what the disciples meant? How is that different from what the world says? (v. 4)

6. Based on Jesus' teaching in verses 5–10, what is our responsibility to each other as believers?

7. Jesus used hyperbole or exaggeration in verses 8–9. What was he saying about the lifelong battle we have against sin?

8. Who did Jesus mean by "little ones" in verse 10? (see Romans 8:16; 1 John 2:1, 28; 1 John 3:1; Galatians 3:26)

9. What do Psalms 91:11–12, Psalms 103:20–22 and Hebrews 1:14 tell us about angels? What does Jesus say about those angels in verse 10 in Matthew?

10. How many sheep have to go astray before the man goes searching? What does the parable in verses 12–14 tell us about Jesus' love and concern for those in His flock who go astray?

11. What gives the man joy? How does this parable teach that Jesus is the Son of God?

Application

Have you ever been the one sheep? How did the Lord draw you back to Himself? Do you know any "wayward sheep?" What part might you play in bringing them back to the fold?

A DEEPER LOOK

Literally cutting off your hand or plucking out your eye will not keep you from sinning. Read the verses below. What does God's Word say can keep you from sinning?

Romans 7:15–25

Colossians 3:1–10

Titus 2:11–14

Are there cherished things in your life that are causing you (or others) to stumble? What do you need to do to cast that aside and treasure Christ instead?

STUDY FIVE
Prayer and Forgiveness

This is a familiar passage for those who have wrestled with forgiving an offense. And we say with Peter, "Show me the limits of mercy. How far does forgiveness have to go?" There is good news and bad news for believers: Jesus does not keep record of our wrongs, and as His disciples, neither should we. This is a real-life picture of what it means to go after a brother or sister who's gone astray. In love, look together at the sin. Widen the circle if he cannot see the fault. If disobedience persists, then sometimes, the greatest act of grace is to withdraw—not in contempt but in firm disconnection. But the goal remains the same: ultimate restoration. Jesus' parable is once again a mirror, reminding the disciples of their position as slaves in debt, and of the merciful authority of the Master they serve, who is their only hope.

Matthew 18:15–35

"**15** 'If your brother sins, go and show him his fault in private; if he listens to you, you have won your brother. **16** But if he does not listen to you, take one or two more with you, so that by the mouth of two or three witnesses every fact may be confirmed. **17** If he refuses to listen to them, tell it to the church; and if he refuses to listen even to the church, let him be to you as a Gentile and a tax collector. **18** Truly I say to you, whatever you bind on earth shall have been bound in heaven; and whatever you loose on earth shall have been loosed in heaven.

19 'Again I say to you, that if two of you agree on earth about anything that they may ask, it shall be done for them by My Father who is in heaven. **20** For where two or three have gathered together in My name, I am there in their midst.'

21 Then Peter came and said to Him, 'Lord, how often shall my brother sin against me and I forgive him? Up to seven times?' **22** Jesus said to him, 'I do not say to you, up to seven times, but up to seventy times seven.

23 'For this reason the kingdom of heaven may be compared to a king who wished to settle accounts with his slaves. **24** When he had begun to settle them, one who owed him ten thousand talents was brought to him. **25** But since he did not have the means to repay, his lord commanded him to be sold, along with his wife and children and all that he had, and repayment to be made. **26** So the slave fell to the ground and prostrated himself before him, saying, 'Have patience with me and I will repay you everything.' **27** And the lord of that slave felt compassion and released him and forgave him the debt. **28** But that slave went out and found one of his fellow slaves who owed him a hundred denarii; and he seized him and began to choke him, saying, 'Pay back what you owe.' **29** So his fellow slave fell to the ground and began to plead with him, saying, 'Have patience with me and I will repay you.' **30** But he was unwilling and went and threw him in prison until he should pay back what was owed. **31** So when his fellow slaves saw what had happened, they were deeply grieved and came and reported to their lord all that had happened. **32** Then summoning him, his lord said to him, 'You wicked slave, I forgave you all that debt because you pleaded with me. **33** Should you not also have had mercy on your fellow slave, in the same way that I had mercy on you?' **34** And his lord, moved with anger, handed him over to the torturers until he should repay all that was owed him. **35** My heavenly Father will also do the same to you, if each of you does not forgive his brother from your heart.'"

1. What is the process of restoration that Jesus described in verses 15–17? Who is the process specifically for?

2. What did Jesus say is the consequence for an unrepentant sinner in terms of community? (v. 17)

3. What does verse 18 mean in this context? In terms of church discipline, how does this speak to or instruct about what's negotiable and what isn't in the body of Christ?

4. Consider again the context of verses 19–20. What would two or three be agreeing or asking about (v. 16–17)? What does this tell us about the authority God gives church leadership? What comfort can we take from this?

5. What does this passage (vv. 21–34) say about our response to the unrepentant believer in verse 17?

6. In light of the discussion in verses 15–20, what was Peter trying to clarify in verse 21? Why might Peter have chosen the number seven?

NOTE: Based on Amos 1:3 and 2:6, rabbis taught that a Jew needed only to forgive a repeated sin three times.

7. Jesus appeared to be giving a mathematical answer. Based on His consistent use of exaggeration in instruction, what was Jesus actually saying?

8. To what did Jesus compare the kingdom of heaven in verse 23?

   • Who was the king?

   • Who are the slaves?

   • What is the debt?

NOTE: Ten thousand talents was like saying "a zillion dollars" — impossible to repay!

   • What is the heart attitude revealed?

9. Where is grace on display in this passage?

10. How do you respond to the question in verse 33? How does this parable teach us to respond to a brother or sister who has offended and is repentant?

Application
Have you ever found yourself on one side or the other in the process described in verses 15–17? How did you respond? What did you learn?

A DEEPER LOOK
Trace the theme of humility in chapter 18.

How does Jesus teach about this heart attitude?

WRAPPING UP
In Revelation 1:12–18, John gives us—under the limitations of language—a picture of Jesus, God's Son. Read this passage and meditate on the picture Scripture gives us of the returning Son of God.

ENDNOTES

Week One:

Sanders, J. Oswald. *The Incomparable Christ*. Chicago: Moody Publishers; New Edition, 2009.

Week Six:

Guzik, David. *Commentary on the Bible*. Matthew 12. EnduringWord.com. 1997.

Week Seven:

Wiersbe, Warren. *Wiersbe's Expository Outlines on the New Testament: Chapter-by-Chapter through the New Testament with One of Today's Most Respected Bible Teachers*. Colorado Springs: David C Cook; New edition. 1992.

Week Eight:

Smith, William. *Smith's Bible Dictionary*. Luke 7. Public domain. 1863.

Wesley, Charles. *And Can It Be?* Public domain. 1738.

TIMELINE FOR THE LIFE OF JESUS

INCLUDED IN PART ONE:

1. Pre-ministry years

The Angel Gabriel appears to Zacharias and foretells the birth of John the Baptist

The Angel Gabriel appears to Mary and foretells Jesus' birth

Mary visits Elizabeth

John the Baptist is born

Jesus is born in Bethlehem

Shepherds visit the manger

Jesus is presented in the temple in Jerusalem

The Wisemen visit Jesus

Jesus' family escapes to Egypt

Jesus' family returns to Nazareth

Jesus astounds priests in the temple at age twelve

John the Baptist begins his ministry

Jesus is baptized

Jesus is tempted by Satan in the wilderness

Jesus returns to the Jordan; John proclaims "Behold the Lamb of God"

Andrew, Peter, Philip, Nathaniel, and perhaps John begin to follow Jesus

Jesus and disciples go to wedding in Cana; Jesus turns water into wine

2. First Year of Ministry (about 29–30 AD)

Passover: Jesus cleanses the temple in Jerusalem (first time)

Jesus meets with Nicodemus

Jesus ministers in Judea

John the Baptist probably arrested at this time

Jesus meets the woman at the well

The royal official's son is healed

Jesus is rejected at Nazareth, His hometown

He calls Andrew and Peter, James and John to be His disciples

He casts out an unclean demon

Jesus heals Peter's mother-in-law

Disciples experience a miraculous catch

He heals a leper

The paralytic is let down through the roof, forgiven, and healed

Matthew is called to be a disciple

3. Second Year of Ministry (about 30–31 AD)

Man healed at the pool of Bethesda in Jerusalem
Jesus proclaims He is equal with the Father
Controversy over the Sabbath with religious leaders
Man with crippled hand healed
The twelve appointed to follow Jesus
Sermon on the Mount given
The centurion's slave is healed
The widow of Nain's son is raised from the dead
Jesus answers John the Baptist's disciples' questions
Jesus curses Chorazin, Bethsaida, and Capernaum
Jesus is anointed by a disreputable woman
The blind-mute demonic spirit is cast out
Kingdom Parables
Calmed the stormy sea
Casts demons out into swine
Healed a woman who was hemorrhaging
Raised Jairus' daughter
Healed two blind men
Cast out demon from a mute and blind man
Taught and rejected again in Nazareth
The twelve disciples sent out
John the Baptist is beheaded
Jesus feeds the five thousand
Jesus appears as a ghost walking on water

4. Third Year of Ministry (about 31–32 AD)

Bread of Life discourse
Jesus withdrew to Tyre and Sidon
The Gentile woman's daughter delivered from demons
Jesus feeds the four thousand
Healed a blind man at Bethsaida
Peter proclaims Jesus is the Christ at Caesarea Philippi
The transfiguration
Demon cast out of boy
Temple tax paid
Teaches on forgiveness

INCLUDED IN PART TWO:

Jesus is ridiculed by His brothers
Journey to Jerusalem
Chief priests and Pharisees try to arrest Jesus
Jesus forgives an adulterous woman
The seventy are commissioned
Parable of Good Samaritan
Jesus visits Mary and Martha
Jesus teaches on prayer, hypocrisy, and wealth
Jesus heals a woman on the Sabbath
Jesus heals a blind man

Blind man excommunicated
Jesus teaches on the good shepherd
Jews tried to stone Jesus
Jesus heals a man with dropsy on the Sabbath
Parables of the lost sheep, lost coin, and lost son
Lazarus dies
Jesus raises Lazarus from the dead
Jesus teaches on the second coming
Jesus heals blind man
Zacchaeus meets Jesus
Jesus arrives in Bethany
(The Passion Week begins)
The Triumphant Entry
Jesus cleanses the temple the second time
Jesus teaches in Jerusalem
Jesus speaks "woes" to the Pharisees
The Olivet Discourse
Judas agrees to betray Christ
(The night before His death)
Washes disciples feet
Institutes the Lord's Supper
The Upper Room Discourse
The Garden of Gethsemane
Jesus is arrested
Tried before Annas
Peter denies Jesus
Tried before Caiaphas
Peter denies Jesus two more times
Judas regrets his betrayal
Jesus tried before Pilate
Jesus tried before Herod
Jesus sentenced by Pilate
Jesus' journey to Golgatha
He is crucified
Joseph of Arimathea takes Jesus' body
The body is placed in a tomb
Angel appears to Mary and Mary at the empty tomb
Peter and John arrive at the empty tomb
Jesus appears to Mary Magdalene
Soldiers report empty tomb
Disciples meet Jesus on road to Emmaus
Jesus appears in the upper room
Jesus appears again in the upper room with Thomas present
Jesus appears in Galilee to the disciples and prepares breakfast
Peter in restored to ministry
Jesus appears to many
Jesus ascends into heaven

Memory Verses for *The Amazing Life of Jesus Christ*, Part One

WEEK 1

JESUS, THE PREEXISTENT CREATOR

"In the beginning was the Word, and the Word was with God, and the Word was God."

JOHN 1:1

WEEK 2

JESUS, GOD-SENT

"He will be great and will be called the Son of the Most High; and the Lord God will give Him the throne of His father David; and He will reign over the house of Jacob forever, and His kingdom will have no end."

LUKE 1:32–33

WEEK 3

JESUS, LAMB OF GOD

"The next day he saw Jesus coming to him and said, 'Behold, the Lamb of God who takes away the sin of the world.'"

JOHN 1:29

WEEK 4

JESUS, THE MESSIAH

"The woman said to Him, 'I know that Messiah is coming (He who is called Christ); when that One comes, He will declare all things to us.' Jesus said to her, 'I who speak to you am He.'"

JOHN 4:25–26

WEEK 5

JESUS, THE HEALER

"When evening came, they brought to Him many who were demon-possessed; and He cast out the spirits with a word, and healed all who were ill. This was to fulfill what was spoken through Isaiah the prophet: 'HE HIMSELF TOOK OUR INFIRMITIES AND CARRIED AWAY OUR DISEASES.'"

MATTHEW 8:16–17

WEEK 6

JESUS, EQUAL TO GOD

"But He answered them, 'My Father is working until now, and I Myself am working.' For this reason therefore the Jews were seeking all the more to kill Him, because He not only was breaking the Sabbath, but also was calling God His own Father, making Himself equal with God."

JOHN 5:17–18

WEEK 7

JESUS, TEACHER OF RIGHTEOUSNESS

"When Jesus saw the crowds, He went up on the mountain; and after He sat down, His disciples came to Him. He opened His mouth and began to teach them . . ."

MATTHEW 5:1–2

WEEK 8

JESUS, THE BURDEN BEARER

"Come to Me, all who are weary and heavy-laden, and I will give you rest. Take My yoke upon you and learn from Me, for I am gentle and humble in heart, and YOU WILL FIND REST FOR YOUR SOULS. For My yoke is easy and My burden is light."

MATTHEW 11:28–30

WEEK 9

JESUS, THE STORYTELLER

"All these things Jesus spoke to the crowds in parables, and He did not speak to them without a parable. This was to fulfill what was spoken through the prophet: "I WILL OPEN MY MOUTH IN PARABLES; I WILL UTTER THINGS HIDDEN SINCE THE FOUNDATION OF THE WORLD.""

MATTHEW 13:34–35

WEEK 10

JESUS, THE LIFE GIVER

"And he who does not take his cross and follow after Me is not worthy of Me. He who has found his life will lose it, and he who has lost his life for My sake will find it."

MATTHEW 10:38–39

WEEK 11

JESUS, THE BREAD OF LIFE

"Jesus said to them, 'I am the bread of life; he who comes to Me will not hunger, and he who believes in Me will never thirst.'"

JOHN 6:35

WEEK 12

JESUS, SON OF GOD

"While he was still speaking, a bright cloud overshadowed them, and behold, a voice out of the cloud said, 'This is My beloved Son, with whom I am well-pleased; listen to Him!'"

MATTHEW 17:5

Notes

Notes

Notes

Notes

Notes

Notes